# The Bacteriological Examination of Drinking Water Supplies 1982

**Reports on Public Health and Medical Subjects No. 71**
**Methods for the Examination of Waters and Associated Materials**

Department of the Environment
Department of Health and Social Security
Public Health Laboratory Service

London   Her Majesty's Stationery Office

© Crown copyright 1983
First published 1983
Third impression 1984

ISBN 0 11 751675 9


(First published 1934 as No. 71 in the DHSS series Public Health and Medical Subjects.
Revised 1939, 1957 and 1969. Copies are no longer available).

# The Bacteriological Examination of Drinking Water Supplies 1982

This Report, which is issued in association with the Public Health Laboratory Service, forms part of the following series:

Methods for the Examination of Waters and Associated Materials
Reports on Public Health and Medical Subjects

The Report has been accepted by the following Departments and Organisations:

Department of the Environment
Department of Health and Social Security
Scottish Office
Welsh Office
Department of the Environment, Northern Ireland
Department of Health and Social Security, Northern Ireland
Public Health Laboratory Service

## Foreword

We commend the fifth edition of "The Bacteriological Examination of Drinking Water Supplies 1982" to all water suppliers, local authorities and laboratories throughout the United Kingdom. This Report has been completely revised by a joint Panel of the Standing Committee of Analysts and the Water Committee of the Public Health Laboratory Service. We acknowledge gratefully all their effort and care in its preparation.

The Report takes into account current legislation and the requirements of Directives of the European Community relating to water quality as well as recent advances in microbiology and water supply practice. As in earlier editions, detailed advice is given on sampling frequencies and procedures, methods of laboratory examination and on interpretation of the results.

We emphasize that close cooperation between all concerned with the wholesomeness of water supplies is essential for the protection of public health. The advice in this Report forms a sound basis for such cooperation, and its recommendations should be followed as carefully as possible.

P. J. Harrop, CB
Second Permanent Secretary
Department of the Environment

Sir Henry Yellowlees, KCB, FRCP, FFCM
Chief Medical Officer
Department of Health and Social Security

Dr. J. E. M. Whitehead, MA, MB, FRCPath, Dip Bact
Director
Public Health Laboratory Service

1983

# CONTENTS

# Preface

The first Report on The Bacteriological Examination of Water Supplies was prepared in 1934 by a small committee under the Chairmanship of the late Dr. Thomas Carnworth with the help of the late Sir Alexander Houston and representatives of the Lister Institute of Preventive Medicine, the London School of Hygiene and Tropical Medicine and the Counties Public Health Laboratories. In 1956, the Public Health Laboratory Service Water Committee assumed responsibility for it. To date, there have been four editions, the last issued in 1969. The Department of the Environment, after becoming responsible in 1973 for all aspects of the water cycle, established the Standing Committee of Analysts to review and keep up to date the methods recommended for water examination in the United Kingdom. In 1975, the National Water Council became associated with this Committee.

The Report has been completely revised on behalf of the Standing Committee of Analysts by a joint Panel*, under the Chairmanship of Dr. G. I. Barrow, consisting of the Water Committee of the Public Health Laboratory Service and microbiologists from Water Authorities. The recommendations take account of current legislation, the requirements of relevant water directives of the European Community, and of comments made by the National Water Council, Water Suppliers, Medical Officers for Environmental Health, Environmental Health Officers, and other interested parties. It also embodies the results of new comparative work on media for the coliform group of organisms in multi-laboratory trials and of recent advances in microbiological and water supply practice.

In the preparation of the Report, the needs and responsibilities of widely different organisations and personnel, both within and outside the water industry in the United Kingdom, have been considered. For this reason, there is some repetition in different sections of the Report, but this will serve to emphasize important points. As before, the rationale of bacteriological examination and the principles underlying the search for faecal indicator organisms instead of for pathogens themselves in assessing the microbiological safety and quality of drinking water supplies are first explained. The interpretation of the results of bacteriological examination is discussed next, followed by the standards of bacteriological quality recommended and the minimum frequency of sampling suggested for routine monitoring. The importance of final disinfection, and the measurement of disinfectant residuals, is stressed. The way in which samples should be taken for microbiological examination is also described in detail. All these sections will be of special interest to Medical Officers for Environmental Health, Environmental Health Officers, engineers and scientists, and to managers and administrators in the water industry. The technical sections, which

---

*The members of the joint Panel are shown at the end of this Report. Those responsible for its preparation, and their affiliation, were: Dr. G. I. Barrow, (Chairman) Public Health Laboratory Service (PHLS): Mr. H. Fennell, Yorkshire Water; Dr. R. D. Gray, PHLS (Deceased); Dr. M. Hutchinson, South West Water; Mr. F. Jones, North West Water; Dr. J. A. Rycroft, PHLS; Miss J. K. Stevens, Thames Water; and Dr. A. E. Wright, PHLS.

describe in detail the bacteriological methods recommended for the detection and enumeration of the various indicator organisms, or groups of organisms, and also certain bacterial pathogens, will be of particular concern to microbiologists. Attention is also drawn to the implications of the Health and Safety at Work Act and to the importance of Codes of safe laboratory practice for bacteriological work.

The main changes in the Report, apart from format and revision of the technical methods, include a recommendation for regular reviews of the quality of potable supplies according to the overall routine coliform results to highlight those supplies particularly in need of attention. Minimum surveillance programmes, based on the size of the population served, are recommended for water suppliers, and attention is drawn to the value of fitting special sampling taps at strategic points in distribution systems. Sources and supplies should be assessed in terms of risk factors and, if necessary, the frequency of sampling changed accordingly. Service reservoirs in particular should receive close attention. The sequence of positive coliform results from routine samples followed by negative results on repeat samples should not be regarded with complacency as it may be an indication of low-level or intermittent contamination. The value of independent random consumer samples taken on behalf of local authorities is reaffirmed and it is recommended that they should continue. Emphasis is placed on the role of the bacteriologist both in an advisory capacity and in investigative work.

Since the last edition of Report 71 was published in 1969, major changes have taken place throughout the United Kingdom in the administrative structure of water supply and sewerage services, local government and the National Health Service, all of which have a bearing on the responsibilities for ensuring that drinking water supplies are wholesome. In England and Wales, Water Authorities were set up in 1974 with direct control of the whole water cycle, the Department of the Environment having overall governmental responsibility and receiving advice on medical and health aspects from the Department of Health and Social Security. At the same time, local authorities relinquished their jurisdiction over water supply and sewage disposal functions, although they remain statutorily responsible for monitoring the 'wholesomeness and sufficiency' of water supplies in their areas. Before 1974, Medical Officers of Health, employed by local authorities, exercised executive responsibility for public health services, including the safety of water supplies. After re-organisation, they were replaced by Medical Officers for Environmental Health with advisory functions, mostly employed by Health Authorities, with day-to-day duties exercised by Environmental Health Officers. Similar changes have taken place in Scotland and Northern Ireland, though the responsible bodies and the titles of the officials vary; for example, in Scotland, Regional and Island Councils are now responsible for water supplies.

Although Chief Environmental Health Officers are responsible for carrying out agreed monitoring programmes on behalf of local authorities and for collating the results, it is emphasized that it is still the responsibility of the Medical Officer for Environmental Health to give advice if there is any microbiological evidence to suggest that a water supply may be unwholesome. Indeed, if microbiological results indicate that the water is unsafe to drink, it is the duty of the Medical Officer for Environmental

Health to advise immediately on any further action and investigation considered necessary. If waterborne infections are suspected, the Medical Officer for Environmental Health must assume executive responsibility and a co-ordinating role for the control of any outbreak of disease. The Medical Officer should usually seek advice from the local public health laboratory, or its equivalent, and if necessary, the assistance of the PHLS Communicable Disease Surveillance Centre. As there have been some difficulties in communication, especially when untoward events have occurred, it is essential that there should be local arrangements at all levels for direct and continuing liaison between those concerned with potable supplies — water undertakings, local authorities and National Health Service authorities, including the Public Health Laboratory Service. The importance of clear lines of communication, both within these organizations and between them, cannot be over-emphasized.

The recent Directive of the European Community on the Quality of Water intended for Human Consumption applies to all water for drinking and food processing, no matter how small the supply and irrespective of whether or not it is privately owned. It would be difficult for water suppliers to exercise effective supervision over many private supplies, or to exercise actual control over changes in water quality occurring within consumers' premises. Such surveillance rests with local authorities through Medical Officers for Environmental Health and Environmental Health Officers.

Despite the use of many different sources for abstraction, public supplies of drinking water in the United Kingdom are safe and of high quality, reflecting the high standards of treatment and safeguards practised by the water industry. The microbiological safety of these supplies has been assured in no small measure by regular monitoring and observance of the recommendations contained in previous editions of Report 71. It is hoped that this revised issue will continue to prove useful not only in the United Kingdom but also internationally.

# The Bacteriological Examination of Drinking Water Supplies 1982

This Report has been prepared with the following objectives:

— To outline the principles on which the bacteriological examination of drinking water is based.

— To recommend the minimum frequency with which potable supplies should be examined bacteriologically to ensure adequate surveillance for health and safety.

— To recommend techniques for sampling and examination to ensure proficiency of laboratory practice and comparability of results.

— To give guidance on interpretation of the bacteriological results.

— To act as a guide to compliance with Directives of the European Community relating to water quality.

The report will be of particular importance to medical and other officers concerned with environmental health as well as to bacteriologists, other scientists, engineers and managers responsible for the quality and safety of water supplies. It should be read in conjunction with "Water Supply Hygiene" which recommends safeguards to be taken in the operation and management of public waterworks (NWC, 1979).

## 1. INTRODUCTION

Almost the whole of the population of the United Kingdom is served by public supplies of drinking water — virtually all of which are disinfected, usually by chlorination. However, in some areas, especially rural, where public piped supplies are economically impracticable, water for drinking may have to be taken from private sources. Although these are considered, this Report is primarily concerned with the bacteriological examination and monitoring of public supplies — not only as the water is distributed, but also as it is collected and treated. Reference is made also to the possibility of inadequacy of treatment, especially following the sudden increase of pollution at source, as well as to contamination within the distribution system.

The objective of water treatment is to produce a final water which is microbiologically and chemically safe for consumption as well as aesthetically acceptable. The range of treatment processes includes storage, flocculation, sedimentation, filtration and disinfection; depending on the source and nature of the water, one or more of these processes is used, each further preparing the water physically and chemically for the essential final stage of disinfection. The treatment and disinfection of water constitute a complex and highly technical field and for further information the following should be consulted: Cox (1969), Skeat (1969), Holden (1970), Hutchinson and Ridgway (1977), and the Standing Committee of Analysts (SCA, 1980). Whilst each of the treatment processes is able to reduce the numbers of micro-organisms, they can never ensure their complete removal and final disinfection is therefore the most important stage of water treatment. As disinfection is the final safeguard against water-borne microbial disease, the dose of disinfectant must be so selected that the chemical demand of the water is satisfied and the desired residual after contact is achieved and maintained throughout the system. It is essential therefore that the disinfectant residuals are monitored regularly. In the United Kingdom chlorination is widely used, and it is important to distinguish between the different forms of chlorine — free or combined — and to check the pH of the water because these and other factors have an effect on the efficiency of disinfection (SCA, 1980). Although micro-organisms differ in their susceptibility to disinfection in decreasing order of resistance — protozoan cysts, bacterial spores, enteroviruses and enteric bacteria — the combination of disinfectant residual and contact time necessary for effective destruction of intestinal viruses and pathogenic bacteria are readily achieved in properly designed and operated treatment works. It should be noted that certain incidents of water-borne disease in the United Kingdom and elsewhere have occurred as a result of inadequate disinfection or because disinfection was not practised (PHLS, 1978). Attention has also been drawn recently to the possible effects of certain chemical compounds formed as a result of disinfection. It is emphasized however that the microbiological safety of potable water supplies is of paramount importance.

Full examination of a water supply embodies four lines of investigation — topographical, chemical, biological and bacteriological — each having its uses and indications and each yielding information not otherwise obtainable. This Report deals with the bacteriological aspects.

Bacteriological examination is particularly important because it still offers the most sensitive test for the detection of faecal and therefore potentially dangerous pollution. Chemical analysis, though lacking the sensitivity of bacteriology in this respect, may nevertheless assist in hygienic assessment, but its major role is in monitoring water supplies for the presence of toxic metals, such as lead and cadmium, as well as for radioactive and other potentially harmful substances. Biological examination is used to detect the presence of algae and animal life which may gain access to supplies through deficiencies in water treatment or because of faults in the distribution network. Topographical examination of catchment areas and water supply networks may reveal potential hazards undetected and undetectable by any other method.

While the proper operation of treatment works is of the utmost importance, frequent bacteriological tests are necessary for adequate assessment of the bacterial purity and safety of drinking water, though chemical and biological tests — apart from those required for treatment control purposes — can be made less frequently. The information derived

2

from bacteriological tests must however be assessed in the light of thorough knowledge of the conditions at the sources of supply, throughout all the stages of treatment to which the raw water may be subjected, and in the distribution system itself.

It is particularly important that the bacteriologist should always bear in mind the many possible contingencies which can result in the sudden pollution of a supply that has previously satisfied all laboratory tests. Failure or inadequacy of treatment processes, particularly disinfection, can be very serious, but there are other hazards that may occur in practice. These include, for example, contamination *via* air-valves and stop-valves, infiltration into mains and service reservoirs, cross-connections with impure water sources and back-siphonage resulting from variations in pressure or temporary cessation of supply. Sudden deterioration in the bacteriological quality of groundwater can occur, for example, through cesspool leakage, from accidental or illicit contamination of the gathering grounds or by polluting material gaining access through faults or fissures in the water-bearing strata. Heavy rains following prolonged drought may aggravate the pollution of water sources and, possibly of even greater consequence, of service reservoirs where the structure is faulty. Increased pumping from wells, perhaps as a result of prolonged drought and consequent greater demand, may also lead to the pollution of previously satisfactory sources. Whenever these or other environmental conditions occur which may pose a hazard to water supplies, the frequency of bacteriological examination should be increased; a series of tests should be made at short intervals, the points of sampling being carefully chosen so that any trouble may be identified quickly and appropriate action taken.

**A single laboratory examination of any water, whether raw or treated and however favourable the result, does not justify the conclusion that all is well and that the supply will remain suitable for drinking purposes.** Contamination is often intermittent and may not be revealed by the examination of a single sample. The impression of security given by bacteriological testing of a water at infrequent intervals may, therefore, be quite false. Indeed the value of bacteriological tests is dependent upon their frequent and regular use. **It is far more important to examine a supply frequently by a simple test than occasionally by a more complicated test or series of tests.** Information gained in the course of time will provide a standard of quality for any particular source of water, any lapse from which must at once arouse suspicion. The most a bacteriological report can prove is that at the time of examination, certain bacteria indicating excremental contamination did or did not grow under laboratory conditions from the sample of the water received and tested. It must be emphasized that, when inspection shows a water supply to be obviously subject to contamination, remedial action should be taken without waiting for and irrespective of the results of bacteriological examination.

Water undertakings have a duty to supply 'wholesome', and therefore safe and aesthetically acceptable, water for drinking. They will doubtless assure themselves of this by implementing a minimum sampling programme as recommended in this Report. Local authorities in England and Wales have statutory duties under the Public Health and Water Acts* to satisfy themselves of the 'wholesomeness and sufficiency' of drinking water supplies in their areas. Although in Scotland and Northern Ireland the legislation is different, the practical effects of the statutory provisions are similar. National Health Service Authorities, though not specifically mentioned, also have a substantial interest in the quality and safety of water supplies. In particular, the Medical Officers who advise local authorities on environmental health still have the responsibility for advising on the wholesomeness or otherwise of water supplied in their districts; liaison between all concerned is therefore essential.

Although the Water Acts do not lay down any legal standards for drinking water in the United Kingdom, the recent Directive of the European Community (1980 b) relating to the Quality of Water intended for Human Consumption specifies both 'maximum admissible concentrations' and 'guideline values' for various microbiological, chemical and other parameters and suggests minimum programmes for sampling based on the volume of water supplied and the population served. These factors have all been taken into account in making the recommendations contained in this Report. The Directive applies with effect from 15 July 1985 to **all** water supplied for drinking or for processing food, whether from public or private sources — no matter how small, unless a delay subject to the health protection and other provisions is granted. It should be noted that, provided the recommendations concerning bacteriological examination and frequency of sampling given in this Report are followed, the most important requirements for bacteriology contained in the Directive will be satisfied. Furthermore, the independent surveillance of public water supplies by local authorities and National Health Service authorities, through their medical and environmental health officers, or their equivalent, provides a valuable additional safeguard, and such random checks of drinking water as made available to consumers are also recommended in this Report. It must be stressed however, that these samples are entirely separate from, and additional to, the sampling programmes of water suppliers. In practice, local authorities will also bear a particular responsibility in future for the surveillance of private supplies. In addition, since the Directive applies to all water for drinking, brief reference is made to the bacteriological examination of particular supplies, such as those on trains, ships and aircraft, and in hospitals, food establishments and similar premises.

---

*The principal legislation is as follows:
Public Health Act 1936,
Water Act 1945,
Water Act 1973,
Public Health (Scotland) Act 1897,
Water (Scotland) Act 1980,
The Public Health (Ireland) Act 1878,
Water and Sewerage Services (Northern Ireland) Order 1973,
The Pollution Control and Local Government (Northern Ireland) Order 1978,
Water Supply and Sewerage (Northern Ireland) Act 1945.

# 2. THE BACTERIOLOGICAL EXAMINATION OF DRINKING WATER : RATIONALE

Contamination by sewage or by human or animal excrement is the greatest danger associated with water for drinking — whether it occurs as the result of inadequate treatment or during distribution. This is because sewage from human or animal sources may contain the causative organisms of many communicable diseases such as typhoid fever, bacterial or amoebic dysentery, giardiasis, infective hepatitis and poliomyelitis. If such contamination is recent and if among the population from which the sewage is derived there are cases or carriers of these or other microbial diseases, some of the living causal agents may be present and the drinking of such water may result in further infections. Animals and birds may also harbour in their gut various organisms pathogenic to man, and the importance of these sources of pollution must not be overlooked. Gulls in particular now pose a serious problem because they may breed on catchments, feed at refuse tips and sewage treatment works, and subsequently roost on water, including uncovered service reservoirs. In addition to the drinking of contaminated water, its use in the preparation of food, which may allow the multiplication of microbial pathogens, also presents obvious dangers.

For several reasons, monitoring for the presence of specific pathogenic bacteria, viruses and other agents in water is impracticable and indeed unnecessary for routine control purposes. Any pathogenic micro-organisms present in water are usually greatly outnumbered by, and in general tend to die out more rapidly than, the normal commensal bacterial flora of the human or animal intestine. Although it may be possible to isolate microbial pathogens from contaminated water, especially when it is heavily polluted, large volumes (several litres) of the water may need to be examined, selective media are required for isolation, and the subsequent identification of the organisms involves biochemical, serological and other tests on pure cultures. Reliance is therefore placed on relatively simple and more rapid bacteriological tests for the detection of certain commensal intestinal bacteria — especially *Escherichia coli* and other coliform organisms — because they are easier to isolate and characterize and because they are always present in the faeces of man and warm-blooded animals, and hence in sewage, in large numbers. The presence of such faecal indicator organisms in a sample of drinking water thus denotes that intestinal pathogens could be present, and that the supply is therefore potentially dangerous to health. There is, however, no absolute correlation between the numbers of *E.coli* or other coliform organisms and the actual presence or numbers of enteric pathogens, nor between the risk of illness occurring and the numbers of *E.coli* present in a given sample. The finding of *E.coli* in a properly treated water indicates the presence of material of faecal origin and thus a potentially dangerous situation, the nature and extent of which is best determined by 'on-site' and laboratory investigations by microbiologists. Conversely, the absence of faecal organisms is an indication that, in all probability, intestinal pathogens are also absent.

If a given supply were to receive a single incident of contamination, for example, from a typhoid carrier, it would probably be two weeks before a case of typhoid fever developed and another week or more before it was diagnosed and reported to the Health Authorities. After this lapse of time, it is improbable that bacteriological examination could demonstrate the presence of typhoid bacteria in the water. If the contamination were repeated or continuous then the chances of finding typhoid organisms would be rather greater, but in practice suspicion would usually fall on the water more as the result of epidemiological than of bacteriological enquiry. Even if examination for pathogenic organisms were practicable it would not really be suitable as a routine test because the concern of the bacteriologist is not so much whether the water does contain pathogenic organisms as whether it could do so. Search for normal faecal organisms thus provides a much greater margin of safety.

The organisms most commonly used as primary bacterial indicators of faecal pollution are the coliform group as a whole, and particularly *Escherichia coli* which is undoubtedly faecal in origin.

Throughout this Report, the term 'coliform organisms' refers to Gram-negative, non-sporing rod-shaped bacteria, capable of aerobic and facultatively anaerobic growth in the presence of bile-salts or other surface active agents with similar growth-inhibiting properties, which are able to ferment lactose with the production of acid and gas within 48 hours at 37°C. They are also oxidase-negative.

Coliform organisms which have the same fermentative properties at 44°C are described as 'thermotolerant'. This term is used in preference to 'faecal coliforms' since not all thermotolerant coliform organisms are faecal in origin.

The term *'Escherichia coli'* refers to thermotolerant coliform organisms which ferment lactose (or mannitol) at 44°C with the production of acid and gas within 24 hours, and which also form indole from tryptophan. *Escherichia coli* also gives a positive result in the methyl-red test, does not produce acetylmethylcarbinol (2 hydroxy-3-butanone) in the Voges-Proskauer test, and cannot utilize citrate as the sole source of carbon.

It should be noted that these are not taxonomic, but practical working definitions used for water examination purposes. Some organisms which taxonomically belong to the coliform group will therefore be missed in water examination. They include both anaerogenic and non-lactose-fermenting strains of coliform organisms, as well as occasional strains of *E.coli* which are not thermotolerant. Such strains are, however, usually outnumbered by those which give typical reactions, so that in practice the interpretation of the results of the coliform test should not be affected. Other organisms, such as aeromonads, which can produce acid and gas from lactose will be regarded as presumptive coliform organisms unless excluded by subsequent confirmatory tests.

The choice of tests in the detection and confirmation of coliform organisms, including *E.coli*, should be regarded as part of a continuous sequence, the extent for any particular sample depending partly on the nature of the water and partly on the reasons for examination. The term 'faecal coliforms' as used in other countries and in water Directives of the European Community is equivalent to 'thermotolerant' coliform organisms. Irrespective of their actual identity, all the members of the coliform group of organisms as defined above, may be faecal in origin and an explanation of their presence must always be sought. If there is doubt as to the faecal nature of the pollution, examination for secondary indicator organisms such as faecal streptococci or *Clostridium perfringens* may sometimes be of value. Faecal streptococci occur normally in faeces, but are usually greatly outnumbered by *E.coli*. If organisms of the coliform group but not *E.coli* are found in a water sample, the presence of faecal streptococci can afford important confirmatory evidence of the faecal nature of the pollution. *Cl. perfringens,* a spore-forming anaerobic organism, also occurs normally in faeces, though in much smaller numbers than *E.coli*. The spores of *Cl. perfringens* are capable of surviving in water for a much longer time than vegetative bacteria such as coliform organisms and faecal streptococci, and they are also more resistant to chlorination. The isolation of *Cl. perfringens* from water thus suggests that faecal contamination has occurred previously, and in the absence of coliform organisms and faecal streptococci, that the contamination occurred at some remote time.

Other micro-organisms, such as those associated with soil and vegetation, also occur naturally in surface waters. Many of these organisms are usually able to survive for long periods in the environment and in the warmer months may multiply considerably. Counts of aerobic organisms which grow as colonies on plates of nutrient agar under defined conditions thus provide a useful means of assessing the performance of water treatment processes. Such colony or plate counts can also provide a general indication of the bacterial content and hence the hygienic quality of water supplies, although the counts themselves have little direct health significance. In practice, changes in the pattern of colony counts of samples from a given supply are usually much more significant than the actual numerical count of any particular sample. Thus a sudden increase in the colony count of water in a supply may give forewarning of more serious pollution. Colony counts, if carried out regularly, are also of particular value when water is used for the large-scale preparation of food and drink. Certain organisms, such as those of the Pseudomonas group, can multiply within the distribution network by using nutrients derived from fixtures and fittings or from organic material in the water itself. However, as far as monitoring drinking water for health and safety is concerned, the usual practice in the United Kingdom is to concentrate on the detection of *E.coli* and other members of the coliform group as the essential primary indicators of faecal and therefore potentially dangerous contamination of potable supplies.

## 3. MICRO-ORGANISMS AND THEIR SIGNIFICANCE

### 3.1 Organisms Indicative of Faecal Pollution

The search for organisms indicative of faecal pollution instead of for pathogens themselves is universally accepted for monitoring the microbial pollution of water supplies. Ideally, the finding of these indicator bacteria should denote the potential presence of intestinal pathogens. Indicator bacteria should be abundant in faeces and sewage; absent or at least very small in number from all other sources; capable of easy isolation, identification, and numerical estimation; and unable to grow in the aquatic environment. They should also be more resistant than pathogens to disinfectants such as chlorine, as well as to environmental stress. In practice, there is no organism which consistently meets all these criteria, but in the United Kingdom, most of them are fulfilled by *E. coli* as the essential indicator of pollution by faecal material of human or animal origin. Other organisms which possess some of these properties can also be used to provide supplementary information in certain circumstances. They include other coliform organisms, faecal streptococci, *Cl. perfringens,* and possibly other intestinal commensals. The particular test or combination of tests to be used in water examination must be left to the discretion of the bacteriologist, as they will depend on the nature of the sample, the actual circumstances and the information required. It is again stressed, however, that it is far more important to examine a water supply frequently by a simple but adequate test than occasionally by a more complicated test or series of tests.

In the United Kingdom, the numbers of indicator organisms present in water are usually estimated either by the "Multiple Tube" method or by the "Membrane Filtration" technique. Both methods have advantages and disadvantages and are subject to statistical variability, but they usually yield similar information in practice. However, it should not be assumed that equivalent results will always occur and, before adopting either method as the main routine procedure, tests should be carried out in parallel to establish their equivalence or the superiority of one method over the other.

In the multiple-tube method, measured volumes of water are added to sets of tubes of a selective enrichment medium, which are then incubated. After incubation, a presumptive count of the indicator organism sought is obtained from probability tables according to the number of tubes showing growth with the appropriate reaction. Further tests are then necessary to confirm that the specific indicator organism is in fact present in each tube showing a positive reaction. The results, both presumptive and confirmed, provide statistical estimates of the most probable number (MPN) of the indicator organism sought likely to be present in 100 ml of the sample of water. In most instances, the 'true' number will lie within a range of approximately one quarter to three times the estimated number. The time required for the complete test varies for different indicator organisms. Although preliminary results may be available within 18 hours, the presumptive stages can take up to 48 hours and confirmation a further 24-48 hours.

In the membrane-filtration technique, a measured volume of water is passed through a sterile membrane which retains micro-organisms at its surface. The membrane is then placed on a suitable medium which, during incubation, allows the indicator organism sought to grow and form characteristic colonies. The number of such colonies provides a direct count of the indicator organism present in the volume of water examined. These colonies can be subcultured to appropriate media for confirmation and, if necessary, further identification. For the coliform test, two volumes of the sample are filtered through separate membranes — one being used to estimate the number of presumptive coliform organisms and the other the number of presumptive *E. coli.* It must be appreciated, however, that replicate membrane tests on a given sample of water could not be expected to yield identical results, and the range of counts thus obtained would lie mainly within statistically calculated upper and lower limits. For this reason, membrane filtration results are estimates, subject to statistical variation, of the numbers of the indicator organism present in the original water. The method requires 18-24 hours for presumptive *E. coli* and other coliform organisms and up to 48 hours for presumptive faecal streptococci and *Cl. perfringens*. Subsequent confirmatory tests normally take a further 24-48 hours. The technical methods for each of the various indicator organisms referred to are described in Section 7. Interpretation of the results of these tests is considered briefly in the following sections.

### 3.1.1 *Escherichia coli* and other Coliform Organisms

*Escherichia coli* is the most abundant coliform organism present in the normal human and animal intestine, occurring in numbers approaching 1000 million ($10^9$) per gram of fresh faeces. It is rarely found in soil, vegetation or water in the absence of excremental contamination. Coliform organisms other than *E. coli* occur in the intestine but their combined numbers seldom exceed one million ($10^6$) per gram of fresh faeces. They are widely distributed on agricultural land treated with manure, and they can also occur in small numbers — seldom more than 100 per gram — in apparently unpolluted soils which are free from *E. coli*. Indeed, some samples of soil have been found to be completely free from coliform organisms. In contrast, small numbers of *E. coli* can sometimes be found in soil far removed from the possibility of faecal contamination by man and domestic animals, and its presence is then attributed to incidental pollution by wild animals or birds. The distribution of other coliform organisms in nature thus suggests that they may all be primarily faecal in origin and that outside the body they can survive longer than *E. coli,* and may even multiply in certain circumstances. For example, jute imported from the tropics — which was previously widely used in the jointing of mains — is often contaminated with an irregular type of coliform organism which has been shown to multiply freely once the jute is immersed in water (Taylor and Whiskin, 1951).

Since *E. coli* and other coliform organisms are present in large numbers in faeces and sewage and can be detected in numbers as small as 1 in 100 ml of water, they are the most sensitive indicator bacteria at our disposal for demonstrating excremental contamination. For this reason not only must coliform organisms, including *E. coli* be detected when present, but estimation must also be made of their numbers in order to assess the degree of pollution and hence danger to health. The test is thus both qualitative and quantitative. In the United Kingdom, the following general propositions apply to the interpretation of the results of the coliform test. The presence of *E. coli* in a water sample always indicates potentially dangerous contamination of either human or animal origin. High counts indicate heavy or recent pollution; low counts, slight or relatively remote pollution. The fact that there is no satisfactory laboratory test to distinguish between *E. coli* of human and of animal origin does not matter in practice since domestic animals, rodents and birds may harbour or carry many organisms pathogenic to man, especially those of the Salmonella group — including *Salmonella paratyphi B*. Moreover, even in the presence of obvious animal sources of pollution, it is usually impossible to be certain that human contamination has not also occurred. Surface waters and reservoirs are particularly liable to pollution from animals and birds, especially gulls. Indeed, salmonella organisms may sometimes be present in surface waters containing few *E. coli*.

9

The presence of *E. coli* even in small numbers must therefore be regarded as indicating the possible presence of intestinal pathogens.

The presence of coliform organisms, but not *E. coli,* in a sample of water may be due to a variety of causes, and the interpretation of such a result is more difficult. For example, the finding of coliform organisms in a water sample may indicate past excremental contamination at a time sufficiently remote to have allowed *E. coli* to die out, or it may herald the onset of more dangerous pollution in the future. In the former instance, frequent testing, had it been carried out, would already have demonstrated the excremental nature of the pollution. In the latter instance, the sudden appearance of coliform organisms in a water supply from which they had previously been consistently absent would indicate new and possibly dangerous pollution. Coliform organisms other than *E. coli* can also occur in water sources as a result of contamination by soil washings or from growth on decaying vegetation, especially in warm weather. In wells, pollution of the shaft or adit may be caused by the presence of old sacking, decayed woodwork, or other material serving as a suitable source of nutrients for bacterial growth even though the underground water itself may be quite pure. In distributed water, growth may occur on all manner of non-metallic materials such as packings, washers and vegetable-based lubricants.

The presence of coliform organisms, however few, in a supply of chlorinated water indicates either inadequate treatment or the access of undesirable material after treatment. The origin of such organisms must always be sought in order to determine whether they are of any sanitary significance. The possibility that coliform organisms may gain access accidentally or inadvertently to the sample during or after collection, as for example from a dirty tap, from the sampler's hands, or from an unsuitable sampling bottle should not be overlooked. An apparently polluted water supply, when properly re-sampled, may be found to be quite satisfactory. However, since intermittent low-level pollution is always possible, occasional unsatisfactory results should not be attributed to errors in sampling and dismissed without adequate investigation.

The laboratory methods for *E. coli* and other coliform organisms are described in Sections 7.7 — 7.9.

### 3.1.2 Faecal Streptococci

Faecal streptococci include a number of different species which occur in man and animals though in varying numbers. In human faeces, they rarely exceed 1 million ($10^6$) per gram and are often much fewer; their numbers are thus normally considerably smaller than those of *E. coli,* although they may occasionally exceed those of the other coliform organisms. In animals, the faecal streptococci present vary with dietary and other factors, but they are generally more numerous than in man, often occurring in numbers exceeding those of *E. coli.* Faecal streptococci do not multiply in water and they are usually more resistant than *E. coli* to environmental stress and as a result survive longer. Some of them may also be more resistant to chlorination than are members of the coliform group of organisms. Faecal streptococci are rarely found in an apparently unpolluted environment.

The species of streptococci in faeces, and therefore those most likely to be found in polluted water, belong to two main groups. The first group includes

*Streptococcus faecalis, Str. faecium* and *Str. durans* which are normally present in man and various animals. The second group, comprising *Str. bovis, Str. equinus* and *Str. avium,* does not usually occur in man. The term 'faecal streptococci' is used to refer collectively to all these named species, as well as to strains of faecal habitat with cultural and biochemical properties intermediate between them, which possess Lancefield's serological group D antigen. Other serologically distinct streptococci occasionally present in faeces include *Str. mitis* and *Str. salivarius* which inhabit the mouth and are swallowed in the saliva. Such strains differ in many respects from true faecal streptococci and their presence in water should not necessarily be regarded as evidence of faecal contamination.

Certain species of faecal streptococci are often associated with particular animals; for example, *Str. bovis* occurs in large numbers in sheep and cattle, *Str. equinus* is mainly associated with horses, and *Str. avium* with poultry and other birds. Although *Str. faecium* is common to man and many animals, *Str. faecalis* is not as abundant in some animals as in man. For these reasons, a differential count of the actual streptococcal species present in water may sometimes help in tracing a source of pollution. The numbers of *E. coli* compared with faecal streptococci in water are used in some countries in an attempt to assess the nature of recent faecal pollution, a high ratio suggesting a human source, and a ratio less than one, an animal source. This kind of numerical approach, however, has limitations because of the many variables, such as time, temperature, pH and the differential survival of organisms as well as the possibility of multiple sources of pollution, which may each affect the validity of the results.

In the United Kingdom, the main value of examination for faecal streptococci lies in assessing the significance of doubtful results from other tests, such as the occurrence of large numbers of coliform organisms in the absence of *E. coli*. In these circumstances, the presence of faecal streptococci always confirms faecal contamination of the water.

The laboratory techniques for faecal streptococci are described in Section 7.10.

### 3.1.3 *Clostridium perfringens*

*Clostridium perfringens,* the most important member of the group of anaerobic sulphite-reducing clostridia, is normally present in human and animal faeces, though usually in numbers much fewer than those of *E. coli* and faecal streptococci, and it is thus less sensitive as a direct indicator of excremental pollution. In normal faeces, it seldom exceeds $10^4$ per gram and in sewage it is present in even smaller numbers. *Cl. perfringens* can form resistant spores which survive in water and in the environment much longer than *E. coli* and other faecal indicator organisms. The spores are therefore very common in manured soil; their occasional presence in areas remote from human habitation is attributed to chance contamination from birds and wild animals. Since the spores of *Cl. perfringens* are not always inactivated by the concentrations of chlorine and contact times normally used in water supply practice, they will sometimes occur in small numbers in treated supplies derived from polluted sources.

In the absence of other faecal indicator organisms, the presence of *Cl. perfringens* in a water source generally implies remote or intermittent faecal pollution, and it is therefore of much less significance in terms of immediate or direct risks to health. It may, however, indicate the need to increase the frequency of sampling of a given source which was previously examined only at infrequent intervals. The presence of *Cl. perfringens* together with coliform organisms, but not *E. coli,* confirms the faecal origin of the pollution. In a treated water, the presence of the spores of *Cl. perfringens* in the absence of *E. coli* known to have been present in the raw water, indicates that the treatment has been effective in removing or inactivating the vegetative cells of indicator organisms, and hence of any potential bacterial pathogens. In these circumstances, the spores of *Cl. perfringens* do not in themselves constitute a direct hazard to health in potable water.

The laboratory techniques for sulphite-reducing clostridia and *Clostridium perfringens* are described in Section 7.11.

## 3.2 Other Micro-Organisms

### 3.2.1 Colony Counts

Water contains a variety of micro-organisms having different optimum temperatures for growth. Most bacteria capable of growth in water will, in laboratory media, do so better at 22°C than at a higher temperature. Organisms which grow best at 37°C usually grow less readily in water and are more likely to have gained access from external sources. Since these two groups of organisms differ in their significance, it is desirable to count them separately. Although colony counts are not strictly comparable with the detection of indicator organisms they are nevertheless used in a similar way to assess the general bacterial quality of water and are therefore considered here briefly.

Colony counts are usually performed in this country by mixing molten agar medium with measured volumes of water in Petri dishes and, after the agar has solidified, incubating some plates at 37°C for 24 or when necessary 48 hours, and others at 22°C for 3 days. The number of colonies that develop in the medium are then counted. These counts do not by any means represent the total number of micro-organisms in the water but simply the number of cells or groups of cells capable of forming visible colonies in the medium used under the cultural conditions specified.

Colony counts are not essential for assessing the safety of potable water supplies, but they are useful for indicating the efficiency of certain processes in water treatment, such as coagulation, filtration, and disinfection, as well as the cleanliness and integrity of the distribution system. They can also be used to determine the suitability of a given supply for the large-scale preparation of food and drink where, to reduce the risk of spoilage, the water should ideally contain few organisms of any kind. The main value of colony counts lies in comparing the results of repeated samples from the same supply, so that any significant change can be detected. Regular examination of water supplies at selected points during treatment and distribution will yield a picture of the range of counts to be expected for a particular supply, any change from which should be viewed with suspicion. A sudden increase, for example, in the count at 37°C in a source from which the counts had previously been consistently low would call for immediate investigation since it might be an early sign of more specific and serious pollution. On the other hand, the count at 22°C is particularly liable to variations related to seasonal, environmental and other factors. Any changes in these counts are usually of little direct significance to health.

The laboratory techniques for colony counts are described in Section 7.12.

### 3.2.2 The Pseudomonas Group

Fluorescent pseudomonads are widespread in the environment and are able to multiply on a wide range of substrates. When these organisms gain access to treated water, they may proliferate in certain circumstances by utilizing nutrients either present in the water or derived from unsuitable materials used in the construction of distribution systems or in domestic plumbing installations.

*Pseudomonas aeruginosa,* an important member of the group, is probably derived from human or animal excrement, but its presence in faeces is not universal. Because of this and its ability to multiply in water containing suitable nutrients, it cannot be used as an indicator of faecal pollution. Its presence, however, in potable waters is undesirable as subsequent growth of this organism is often associated with considerable deterioration in bacterial quality. This may affect the colour, turbidity, taste and odour of the water, and result in consumer complaints. Deterioration of this kind is particularly liable to occur, for example, where there is limited flow in part of the distribution system, and also a rise in the temperature of the water. Other fluorescent pseudomonads, especially *Ps. fluorescens* and *Ps. putida,* may also give rise to problems in treated waters by producing slimes during growth which form the basis of consumer complaints. Since these organisms can grow in so many different situations, it is impracticable to give any guarantee about their absence from distributed water — however desirable this may be — although they should not normally be present in water for drinking as it leaves the treatment works. In the United Kingdom, the enumeration of fluorescent pseudomonads, and *Ps. aeruginosa* in particular, is therefore **not** recommended as a routine procedure, although it may be of value in the investigation of consumer complaints and distribution problems. It may also be of value within certain industries — as for example in the manufacture of food, drink or pharmaceutical products — where water of exceptional bacterial purity is often required. In hospitals and other places where debilitated persons are particularly prone to infection, *Ps. aeruginosa* may be of some importance as an opportunist pathogen and its presence in water may thus be of concern. In such situations, where water free from *Ps. aeruginosa* is desirable, special treatment facilities may be required on site. For all these reasons, methods suitable for the detection and enumeration of *Ps. aeruginosa* in water are given in Section 7.13, although it is emphasized that monitoring potable supplies for *Ps. aeruginosa* is not recommended as a routine.

### 3.2.3 Nuisance Organisms

These organisms can cause objectionable tastes, odour, colour and turbidity in water and may interfere with treatment processes by blocking strainers and filters. They constitute a morphologically and physiologically diverse group which includes fungi, actinomycetes, iron and sulphur bacteria, algae and

13

protozoa. Most of them are controlled by the usual water treatment processes, but occasionally they may establish themselves in sediments, slimes and on materials within the distribution system (Hutchinson and Ridgway, 1977). Routine examination for such organisms is not recommended because of their diverse nature and unpredictable occurrence.

## 3.3 Pathogenic Organisms

Water undertakings are required to supply 'wholesome' and thus safe water for drinking, and it is with this objective in view that the water supply part of the hydrological cycle is controlled. Instead of routine monitoring by direct examination for the presence of specific pathogens, reliance is placed on frequent, rapid and relatively simple bacteriological tests for the detection of faecal indicator organisms, especially for the control of the final treatment and distribution of potable water. However, for some purposes, such as the management of gathering grounds or the verification of compliance with Directives of the European Community, it may be necessary to carry out direct examination for certain pathogens, notably salmonellae. For this reason, methods for their isolation and enumeration are given in Section 8.

Attention has been drawn recently to the possibility that some viruses, because of their greater resistance to disinfection than bacterial indicator organisms, could survive treatment and might occur occasionally in small numbers in potable supplies. Although the number of virus particles required to cause infection is generally considered to be much lower than that of bacterial pathogens, there is no evidence available in the United Kingdom to suggest that any clinical viral infections have ever been associated with water shown by bacteriological tests to have been adequately treated and disinfected. The routine examination of potable water for viruses is therefore not recommended. However, further information about the fate of viruses in the water cycle, especially their removal by water treatment processes in different situations, would be useful, as would similar work for protozoan pathogens such as Giardia.

## 4. STANDARDS OF BACTERIOLOGICAL QUALITY

In the United Kingdom, there are obligations under Water and Public Health legislation for water undertakings to supply wholesome water, and for local authorities to monitor the wholesomeness and sufficiency of supplies in their areas. In order to fulfil these obligations, guidance is given in this Report on the bacteriological aspects of water quality and hygiene. The recommendations given are not 'standards' in the legal sense of the word but recommended guidelines which, with the experience, professional judgement and common-sense of water engineers, scientists, and public health officials, may be used to assess the bacteriological quality and hence the wholesomeness and safety of water supplies. These recommendations are also in keeping with those of other bodies, including the World Health Organisation (WHO 1971) and the European Community (1980b).

In the assessment of the bacteriological quality of drinking water, the stage of supply must always be taken into account. Water undertakings are responsible for the quality of water entering supply. From this point onwards, the water is subject to contamination or deterioration within the distribution system although the responsibility of the water undertaking continues as far as the curtilage of the consumer's property or other defined boundary. Beyond this point, the water is also subject to contamination or deterioration within the plumbing installations of the properties, but water undertakings can have only limited, if any, practical responsibility for this other than through Byelaws. Indeed, it would be extremely difficult for them to exercise effective control over the quality of the water at the consumer's tap. For adequate control of the quality of water in supply, it is therefore necessary to take samples from carefully selected sites. The examination of a single sample can indicate no more than the conditions prevailing at the time of sampling at that particular point in the supply, and it cannot be stressed too strongly that bacteriological examination has its greatest value when it is repeated frequently. Recommendations are given in this Report about the location and number of sites and the minimum frequency of sampling needed to satisfy these requirements.

## 4.1   Water Entering the Distribution System

Most public supplies of drinking water derived from surface sources in the United Kingdom undergo at least some form of clarification, and all of them should be disinfected before distribution. Ground waters, which do not normally need clarification, should also be disinfected. Efficient treatment culminating in disinfection, usually by chlorination, should yield a water free from any coliform organisms no matter how polluted the original water may have been. **In practice, this means that in all waters intended for drinking, no coliform organisms should be detectable in any sample of 100ml.** It should be the aim of every undertaking to produce water of this quality at all times. If any sample of water entering the distribution system shows deviation, no matter how small, from this standard, an immediate and thorough investigation is required. In the testing of chlorinated waters, it is important that all positive presumptive coliform results, whether from tubes or membrane filters, should be verified by appropriate confirmatory tests to exclude false-positive reactions.

## 4.2   Samples from the Distribution System

Water which is of excellent quality when it enters the distribution system may undergo some deterioration before it reaches the consumer's tap. Coliform organisms, for example, may gain access through air valves, hydrants, booster pumps, defective service reservoirs, cross-connections, back-siphonage, and faulty appliances, or through unsatisfactory repairs to plumbing installations. Coliform organisms may also occur in, and multiply on, materials used in construction — such as valve packings, lubricants and tap washers. Contamination of an excremental nature that gains access to the water in supply is at least as dangerous as the distribution of initially polluted and inadequately treated water. Although coliform organisms associated with materials used in construction may have little or no sanitary significance, there is no certain way of determining their source without detailed investigation. Accordingly, any indication of contamination, no matter how small, must be investigated further.

15

**Ideally, all samples taken from a distribution system, including those from consumers' premises, should be free from coliform organisms.** However, for the reasons already given, this is not always attainable in practice, and tolerance may be allowed up to the following limits for routine samples:

— *E. coli* should not be detectable in any sample of 100 ml,

— no sample of 100ml should contain more than three coliform organisms,

— coliform organisms should not be detectable in any two consecutive samples of 100ml from the same or a closely related sampling point,

— for any given distribution system, coliform organisms should not occur in more than five per cent of routine samples, provided that at least 50 samples have been examined at regular intervals throughout the year.

When **any** coliform organisms are found, the minimum action necessary pending confirmation is to check that the disinfection process is operating satisfactorily, and to re-sample immediately from the same point: additional samples should also be taken from other related sites in order to confirm the coliform result and help to locate the probable source of contamination. It must be stressed that, because serious consequences can follow contamination, it is essential for the bacteriologist to initiate any other action and investigation considered necessary, including on-site inspection and sampling. Since the apparent number of coliform organisms present is subject to sampling and other inherent variables, interpretation of quantitative results may be difficult for those not fully conversant with the methods employed. With a continuous record of results extending over a period of at least one year and knowledge of the water treatment processes used and the distribution conditions prevailing at the time, water scientists must decide whether any departure from the usual quality for the particular supply is significant or not. Satisfactory results obtained on repeat samples taken after the detection of coliform organisms in a routine water sample should not be regarded with complacency. The recurrence of such findings in any particular supply may be indicative of low-level contamination. In these circumstances, further investigation of the supply is essential, and the frequency of routine sampling should be increased or larger volumes of the water examined. The possible value of colony counts could also be considered.

The persistence of coliform organisms in successive samples or the appearance of *E. coli* indicates that undesirable material is gaining access to the water and that measures should be taken at once to ascertain and remove the source of contamination. As an additional safeguard to health, it may be necessary to increase the concentration of residual chlorine in the supply. This is especially relevant in the case of contaminated service reservoirs. In particular, it is more important to increase the dose of disinfectant until the problem is overcome and accept any ensuing taste complaints than to allow the risks to public health from microbial contamination to persist.

# WATER BACTERIOLOGY

AB (S. water)
  Membrane counts on teepol broth
  Indicator: yellow counts = coliforms
  Plates (1ml), 37°C + 22°C - counts.
  Isolate yellow colonies → 44°C + re-check.
  Growth at 44°C → confirm
  Sampling - add thio to ↓ Cl and )
  enable bac growth.

## 4.3 Reviews of the Quality of Water in Distribution Systems

It is recommended that the results of coliform tests on **all** routine samples taken from water in distribution should be reviewed periodically and at least annually. Although individual samples represent the water at the time and place of sampling, if sufficient have been taken, the results may be used to give a general indication of the standard of bacteriological quality of the supply, or part of the supply related, for example, to a particular service reservoir. The purpose of these reviews is to enable water undertakings and health officials to identify problem areas, including any seasonal variations. It is emphasized that they are based on the results of coliform tests on **routine samples only;** repeat samples taken to investigate a particular routine result which was unsatisfactory should **not** be included. In practice, several repeat samples may be needed in such an investigation and inclusion of these results would add bias to the review of that system. For the same reasons, samples arising from special surveys or from complaints by consumers should not be included. The information may be conveniently recorded in the form of charts or graphs so that all the coliform results can be assessed continuously. In reviewing them, account should be taken of abnormal weather or other conditions during sampling. The detection of *E. coli* or other coliform organisms in any routine sample is an unsatisfactory result, and whenever this has occurred, the full circumstances at the time as well as the subsequent investigations and actions taken should be recorded. If there is no satisfactory explanation and if the presence of *E. coli* or other coliform organisms recurs, then the frequency of sampling of that supply should be increased immediately, in addition to any other action taken.

The quality of potable supplies during the period under review may be assessed according to the criteria shown in Table 1, provided that the coliform results from a minimum of about 50 routine samples taken throughout the system are available; the more samples examined, the greater the degree of reliance which may be placed on the overall assessment.

A supply, or part of it, may be regarded as having been excellent during the review period if *E. coli* and other coliform organisms were not detected in any sample.

The supply may be regarded as having been satisfactory during the period if not more than 3 coliform organisms were present in any sample, provided that (a) the presence of *E. coli* was not detected (b) coliform organisms were not found in two or more consecutive samples from the same or from closely related sampling points and (c) coliform organisms were present in not more than five per cent of the samples.

The supply, or the relevant part of it, should be regarded as having been unsatisfactory during the period under review if (a) *E. coli* was present in any sample (b) 10 or more coliform organisms occurred in any sample (c) coliform organisms occurred in two or more consecutive samples from the same or closely related sampling points in the system, or (d) if coliform organisms were present in more than five per cent of the samples.

The presence of more than 3 but less than 10 coliform organisms within the five per cent tolerance limit for routine samples, especially from associated

17

## Table 1. Periodic Quality Reviews of Water Supplies*

| Quality of Supply | Results from Routine Samples | | Tolerance |
| | Coliform count per 100 ml | E. coli count per 100 ml | |
| --- | --- | --- | --- |
| 1 Excellent | 0 | 0 | In all samples |
| 2 Satisfactory | 1 — 3 | 0 | provided that coliform organisms do not occur in consecutive samples or in more than 5 per cent of samples |
| 3 Intermediate | 4 — 9 | 0 | |
| 4 Unsatisfactory† | 10 **and/or** 1 or more<br><br>**or** any coliform organisms present in consecutive samples<br><br>**or** presence of any coliform organisms in more than 5% of routine samples | | In any sample |

Notes

*These quality reviews can be used for supplies only when sufficient results are available from the distribution system during the period under review. In practice a minimum of about 50 routine samples, taken regularly throughout one year, is required. Water entering the distribution system should always be excellent in quality.

†The full circumstances, including the duration and extent of the unsatisfactory coliform results in this category, should be described in the reviews.

sampling points, is of intermediate significance and the results, although not necessarily indicative of an unsatisfactory supply, should not be regarded with complacency. Smaller supplies which are sampled at say less than weekly intervals, such as in rural areas, cannot be regarded as satisfactory with the same degree of reliance even if E. coli and other coliform organisms were absent from every sample. However, at the discretion of water undertakings, such supplies may still be regarded as in keeping with the Directive of the European Community on Water intended for Human Consumption provided that coliform organisms do not occur in more than five per cent of the samples. With very small supplies, the frequency of routine sampling cannot be expected to be sufficient to justify classification on bacteriological grounds alone and their suitability should be judged in part on topographical examination. Indeed, in assessing every supply, account must be taken of the risks of contamination inherent in both the source and the system.

## 4.4  Private Supplies

Where a public water supply may be economically impracticable and reliance has to be placed on small private supplies, it may be difficult to attain the satisfactory standard of bacterial quality in category 2, but such a standard should be the minimum objective. Statutory water undertakings have no jurisdiction over the quality of private water supplies in their area and these private supplies must therefore remain the responsibility of the Medical and Environmental Health Officers of local authorities. In some rural areas, private water supplies may be so numerous that routine monitoring is not practicable. In such circumstances suspicion is most likely to fall on individual supplies as the result of complaints about the water, or illness within the household. The initiation of bacteriological tests of such a water supply would be the responsibility of the local authority health officials. Private water supplies are normally of such limited distribution that, if polluted, they do not constitute a health hazard to the general population. On estates, holiday sites and other establishments with large private supplies, there should be local agreement on the need for special priorities for sampling. Owners of private water supplies should be encouraged to take every measure possible to prevent the access of pollution to the water. Simple methods, such as the removal of obvious sources of contamination from the catchment area, by fencing, and by attention to the coping, brick-lining and covering should reduce the coliform content of even a shallow well or spring to less than 10 coliform organisms per 100 ml. Persistent failure to achieve this, especially when *E. coli* is repeatedly present, should, as a general rule, lead to condemnation of the supply, or at least to the introduction of reliable methods of disinfection.

## 4.5  Water Supplies for Particular Locations

Ideally, the standards of bacteriological quality recommended should apply at the point of use to all water supplied for drinking, food processing or for special purposes. However, the direct responsibility of water undertakings ends at the highway or property boundary, although beyond this point, marked changes in water quality may take place. For example, bacterial growth may occur on filters and in water softeners. Prolonged storage at raised ambient temperatures, together with the use of unsuitable materials of construction within the plumbing system, may also give rise to increased microbial growth including that of coliform organisms. To reduce this problem in the long term, a scheme has been introduced (NWC 1981a) for the testing and approval of materials and fittings used in contact with potable water, with particular reference to their potential ability to support the growth of micro-organisms (BSI 1982). Water suppliers may use this information with advantage in their Byelaws.

It is not practicable to set numerical limits on the colony counts of water in supply, although these can be a valuable guide to the location and degree of deterioration in water quality. A considerable increase in the colony count of say 10 to 100 fold over previous results requires investigation and possibly remedial action. This is most important for example, when potable water is supplied in ships, trains and aircraft as well as in hospitals, food-manufacturing and catering establishments. Local authorities should include such locations in their programmes for environmental monitoring. This will accord with the regulations of the European Community which apply at the point of use to all water intended for drinking or for processing food.

## 4.6 Emergency Procedures

In emergencies, as for example with failure of chlorination, untreated and therefore potentially dangerous water may gain access to the distribution system. To render such water safe for drinking, it is necessary only to bring it to the boil and allow it to cool in clean covered containers (NWC, 1981b). Water so disinfected should be used for all drinks, cleaning teeth and washing salad vegetables. The decision to advise the public to boil water, or to give other guidance, should be taken after consultation with a senior bacteriologist, and preferably also with reference to the Medical and Environmental Health Officers of the local authorities concerned. If for any reason this cannot be done immediately, they should be informed as soon as possible afterwards. The establishment of close liaison between designated officers of water undertakings and local authorities, as well as the Public Health Laboratory Service, is recommended.

In other circumstances, as for example when very high nitrate concentrations occur, an alternative supply of drinking water may be needed for the preparation of infant feeds. If this water is supplied in bottles, it must be of potable quality, and in addition should not contain *Ps. aeruginosa* in samples of 250 ml (European Community, 1980a,b).

It should be noted that bottled natural mineral waters are not within the scope of this Report. They are subject to other regulations, including a Directive of the European Community (1980a), although for microbiological examination, the methods given in this Report may be used.

## 5. FREQUENCY OF SAMPLING FOR BACTERIOLOGICAL EXAMINATION

The frequency of bacteriological examination and the location of sampling points should be such as to ensure control over the hygienic quality of the water supplied. Moreover, it is implicit in the standards recommended that assessment of the bacterial quality of the water should depend not only on the nature and numbers of any coliform organisms found, but also on the number of occasions on which the supply has been examined during the preceding year.

The frequency with which routine monitoring samples should be taken depends, *inter alia,* on the quality of the water at source, the treatment processes applied, the volume of water distributed, the stage of supply, the size of the population served and hence the potential risks to health as well as any local circumstances which may affect these factors. It is clearly more important to take samples of water entering or within the distribution system from locations such as service reservoirs, other water-holding structures, either above or below ground, or from consumers' premises than to sample the water at source or during the various stages of treatment. Nevertheless, the latter samples are often necessary because they do have an important role in process control. It is therefore not possible to specify for every situation how many and how often samples should be taken; this should be left to specialist staff in water undertakings and local authorities. However, the following suggestions for monitoring supplies of drinking water for coliform organisms are given for guidance. This frequency should be increased in the light of any known risk.

## 5.1  Routine Samples

### 5.1.1  Treated Water entering the Distribution System

In principle, the bacteriological monitoring of water at each point of entry to the distribution system should be carried out each day. In addition to regular bacteriological monitoring of water entering supply, the chlorine residual should be measured frequently, and preferably recorded continuously. With most large supplies both these requirements should be fulfilled. However, with small supplies serving a population of about 10,000 or less, daily sampling may not be practicable and reliance must therefore be placed on control of the chlorine residual, with periodic checks on the bacteriological quality of the water at, say, weekly intervals. With larger works, the sampling frequency should be increased in relation to size up to once each day. The efficiency of chlorination is best checked by means of residual chlorine recorders preferably fitted with automatic control or alarm systems. This is particularly important for those stations which are not manned for 24 hours each day, where the residual — both free and total available chlorine — in water leaving the treatment plants should be checked and recorded at least once each day.

From their history, some supplies, as indicated by frequent and regular examination, are known to be consistently of excellent bacteriological quality. This may be because the source is sound and well-protected, or because highly sophisticated treatment processes are used with built-in automatic control and safety procedures. Provided that these supplies are free from foreseeable risks of contamination, such as sewers in close proximity to boreholes or abstraction points, and where the source is consistently of excellent bacterial quality, the water supplier may consider reducing the frequency of bacteriological examination from daily to a minimum of say twice per week. If the source is not consistently of excellent bacterial quality but disinfection operates according to the 'fail-safe' principle, with adequate standby equipment installed, a similar reduction in the frequency of examination may also be considered. This would allow greater effort to be directed towards supplies of doubtful quality.

## 5.1.2 Treated Water within the Distribution System

Water is subject to contamination and deterioration during distribution and it is essential to examine an adequate number of samples commensurate with this hazard. The number of samples should take account of the special risks associated with each supply as well as seasonal factors which could jeopardize the safety of any particular supply. In general, the number of samples required should be based on the size of the population served since, with large populations, there will be a proportionate increase in the complexity of the distribution system and hence in the risks of contamination from causes such as cross-connections and back-siphonage. With very large populations, however, the intervals between successive routine samples taken from different locations in the same part of the distribution system will be minimal. **As a guide, for populations up to 300,000 served by a single supply, it is recommended that one sample per 5000 of the population should be examined each month and that these samples should be taken regularly throughout the period. Where a supply serves a population greater than 300,000, the additional sampling required may be at the reduced rate of 1 per 10,000 of the population per month, with a further reduction to 1 sample per month per 20,000 of the population in excess of 500,000.** In applying these recommendations, there is a need to monitor special features such as service reservoirs and break-pressure tanks because they are particularly liable to contamination. They should preferably be examined weekly, but at least once each month, with samples from different service reservoirs related to a particular supply being taken uniformly throughout the period. Each service reservoir and its associated distribution network should be considered as a separate part of the supply; where practicable they should be sampled on different occasions so as to enhance surveillance of the whole system.

In large conurbations, there is also need for some flexibility over the sampling requirements so as to take particular account of multi-occupancy, high rise and other buildings where pumps, storage tanks and long pipe runs, as well as lack of disinfectant residuals, may present significant risks to the microbiological quality of the water received by consumers. Although these pumps and storage tanks are often situated beyond the curtilage of such properties — and thus technically outside the control of the water supplier, there should nevertheless be agreement between the local authorities and water undertakings concerned on the monitoring programme. This would include, for example, the choice of strategic sampling points and apportionment of the responsibility for collection and laboratory examination of samples as well as joint consultation on any remedial action that may be needed to safeguard the supply as used.

It is the responsibility of water suppliers to collect and examine samples from distribution systems, and to keep Medical and Environmental Health Officers of local authorities informed of the quality of the water distributed in their areas. There should be local liaison and interchange of information on complaints, unsatisfactory samples and any incidents, including repairs, which might affect the quality of the water in supply. The tradition by which local authorities also arrange for the independent collection and testing of samples of drinking water is a valuable check on the safety of supplies and should be encouraged. Close co-operation should ensure that unnecessary duplication of work is avoided.

22

### 5.1.3 Treatment Control Samples

Samples of the raw water at source, or water at various stages during treatment, are often required for process control. Their numbers, frequency and location should be left to the discretion of the water scientist. With borehole supplies, it is important to examine samples of the raw water periodically in order to assess the bacterial quality prior to disinfection; otherwise the possibility of new or increased pollution at source might be masked by disinfection and thus go unnoticed.

During the commissioning of a new supply, especially a well or spring, samples should be collected relatively frequently and under differing weather conditions so that any variation in the bacterial quality of the water can be observed. It is not possible to assess the quality or indeed safety of such supplies without adequate monitoring. When water undertakings carry out pumping-tests on new wells, it is advisable to take several samples related to increased pumping rates because unsatisfactory bacteriological results are more likely to occur during periods of maximum abstraction.

## 5.2 Special Samples: Consumer Complaints

In the event of complaints from consumers about the quality of the water, samples should be taken for investigation including, where relevant, bacteriological examination. These samples should be separate from, and additional to, the general sampling programme of surveillance. In the event of an unsatisfactory result, further samples should be taken from selected points to help to elucidate the problem. These additional samples should not be included in the periodic review statistics for the supply as a whole since they would add undue bias. In taste and odour complaints, the temperature of the water may provide useful additional information.

## 5.3 European Community : Requirements of Water Directives

In the United Kingdom, there has not previously been a legal requirement to monitor the quality of raw water, although for the development of new resources as well as for process control this has invariably been done: it was regarded as no more than good practice. The European Community (1975, 1979) now requires Member States to take measures to ensure that sources of surface water intended for abstraction for water supply conform to certain specified limits. These relate to three categories of water quality which in turn determine the methods of treatment to be applied. The microbiological parameters specified, which include both primary and secondary faecal indicator organisms as well as salmonellae, are 'Guide values' only and are not mandatory. As the competent body, each water undertaking will be responsible for ensuring that all sources of abstraction and the treatment processes applied conform with these requirements. Classification into these categories must be based on an adequate programme of monitoring which should take into account the volume of water abstracted, the population served and the degree of risk engendered by the quality of the water, including the effects of seasonal variations on these factors.

The Directive relating to the Quality of Water intended for Human

Consumption also specifies certain microbiological requirements. Apart from recommending initial quality assessment of new sources, it cites four categories for the routine monitoring of supplies, each with specified minimum sampling frequencies, as well as guidance on the parameters to be considered. These monitoring categories are based on the volume of water produced and the size of the population served, except for small supplies where the frequency of examination is left to the discretion of the national authorities concerned. For microbiological purposes, 'minimum' monitoring (C1) may be regarded as the smallest number of samples required for routine control purposes and 'current' monitoring (C2) as that required for reassurance of hygiene and safety. Together, 'minimum' and 'current' monitoring are in keeping with traditional water supply control and public health practice in the United Kingdom. In the same way, 'periodic' (C3) and 'occasional' (C4) monitoring relate essentially to additional investigations which might need to be carried out by water suppliers if particular difficulties occur unexpectedly or if there are known to be long-standing problems: in either of these circumstances local assessment is essential, during which any tests thought necessary would be done. The overall impact of these microbiological aspects of the Directive thus reaffirms the value and role of traditional British practice as described in this Report.

Where 'periodic' (C3) and 'occasional' (C4) monitoring may apply, the Directive gives 'maximum admissible concentration' values for secondary faecal indicator organisms. Depending on the method used, faecal streptococci should not be detectable in sample volumes of 100ml, and for sulphite-reducing clostridia not more than one should be present in 20ml. In the United Kingdom, it is emphasized, however, that to investigate unexpected or persistent problems, all relevant tests should be done by water suppliers, including if necessary those for supplementary faecal indicator organisms. There is no obligation for water suppliers or local authorities in the United Kingdom to examine **routine** samples for the presence of either faecal streptococci or sulphite-reducing clostridia. Indeed, as indicated in Section 3, the presence in routine samples of either or both of these organisms would only serve to confirm that the supply is subject to pollution. For the 'minimum' monitoring (C1) of treated water, the Directive indicates that, in addition to examination of routine samples for thermotolerant (faecal) coliform organisms*, colony counts at both 37° C and 22° C may be done instead of tests for the total numbers of coliform organisms. In the United Kingdom, however, it is reaffirmed that tests for both *E. coli* and other coliform organisms should always be performed as a routine. If thought necessary for particular reasons, colony counts may be done in addition. For colony counts on such samples the Directive also suggests as target values 'Guide levels' of not more than 10 micro-organisms per ml at 37° C and 100 per ml at 22° C. Although some supplies in the United Kingdom usually meet these values, there are many which will be unable to do so, and British practice, as indicated in Section 3, is based on the philosophy that significant changes in the usual counts for a given supply are far more important than

---

*'Faecal coliforms' are equivalent to 'thermotolerant coliform organisms' as defined on page 6. For water examination purposes in the United Kingdom, the term 'faecal coliform' is regarded as a misnomer since some organisms which accord with the definition are not necessarily of faecal origin.

absolute numbers. It is recommended however, that any colony counts on routine samples from individual supplies which fail to meet these guide levels should be evaluated in the light of local circumstances, including public health considerations and economic practicability.

For current monitoring (C2) of water supplies, the Directive also specifies minimum requirements for colony (plate) counts*. These range from 6 samples per year for a supply serving a population of 10,000 and increase approximately in the proportion of 1 colony count for every 10 routine samples submitted for coliform tests up to 72 samples for a population of 300,000 persons. Thereafter the annual frequency may be reduced such that a minimum of 120 samples should be examined for a population of 500,000, and 240 samples for a single supply serving a population of 1,000,000 or more. To satisfy these requirements for colony counts, the water supplier may examine samples taken at any point during distribution between the treatment works and the consumers' taps. For effective evaluation, however, colony counts need to be done regularly and frequently so that significant changes can be detected from the seasonal norm for a given sampling point in any particular supply. Since water sources and supplies vary considerably in their characteristics throughout the United Kingdom, it is neither desirable nor practicable to specify the need for, the extent of, or the frequency with which colony (plate) counts should be performed on routine samples. This decision must depend on microbiological assessment of each supply, taking account of local circumstances, including the nature of the source, as well as the sampling requirements of the Directive. For the same reasons it is impracticable to specify numerical limits for colony counts, especially those at 22°C, applicable to all supplies. In general they should however be as low as is reasonably practicable. For colony counts, incubation periods of 72 hours for the test at 22°C and 48 hours for that at 37°C are implied in the Directive; for the latter, however, the usual practice in the United Kingdom, as described in Section 7.12, is to count the colonies formed after 24 hours at 37°C. Where necessary, incubation may be continued at 37°C for a further period of 24 hours and the colonies counted again.

For potable water supplied in bottles₍ or other closed containers, the Directive specifies 'Maximum Admissible Concentration' values for colony counts on production samples of not more than 20 micro-organisms per ml at 37°C and 100 per ml at 22°C. As 'Guide values', the water samples should preferably yield colony counts of not more than 5 micro-organisms per ml at 37°C and 20 per ml at 22°C. In addition, these samples must be examined within 12 hours of bottling, and the responsibility for arranging for these tests to be done must therefore rest with the processors. Although the frequency with which samples should be examined is not stated in terms of bottles produced, it is recommended that they should be sufficient to ensure adequate control over the hygiene of the bottling process. In the United Kingdom, it is

*

| No. of samples required | Population (thousands) | | | | | | | |
|---|---|---|---|---|---|---|---|---|
| | <10 | 10 | 50 | 100 | 150 | 300 | 500 | ≥1,000 |
| Annual | † | 6 | 12 | 24 | 36 | 72 | 120 | 240§ |
| Monthly | † | | 1 | 2 | 3 | 6 | 10 | 20§ |

†At discretion          §Should be increased if possible

recommended that *Ps. aeruginosa* should not be detectable in samples of the product in containers as supplied to the consumer. If any samples yield results which exceed the maximum admissible values, the operation and hygiene of all the processes concerned, including the source of the water, should be investigated.

For microbiological purposes, the Directive further states that water intended for use in food- or drink-manufacturing establishments should be examined at least once each year for primary and supplementary faecal indicator organisms. In general, *E. coli,* other coliforms organisms and faecal streptococci should not be detectable in sample volumes of 100ml, and sulphite-reducing clostridia should not exceed 1 per 20ml. To avoid microbial spoilage of certain products, it is advisable for the manufacturers to monitor the microbiological quality of the water actually in use, as water suppliers cannot be responsible for any changes in water quality which occur within such premises. Indeed, many processes in the food and drink industry require water of exceptional microbiological purity and the potable water supplied may thus need further treatment. However, the responsibility for ensuring that the microbiological provisions of the Directive are met must rest jointly with the Environmental Health Departments of local authorities and the manufacturers themselves.

Provided that the monitoring programme recommended for the bacteriological examination of water as set out in this Report is followed by water undertakings and local authorities, the most important minimum requirements of the Directive will be more than satisfied. All that may remain is to provide a special check for certain pathogenic organisms — notably salmonellae — if this should be considered necessary by water suppliers. It is however again stressed that in the United Kingdom it is considered far more important to examine a supply frequently by simple but effective tests for primary organisms indicative of faecal pollution than occasionally by other tests or series of tests as would be necessary for faecal streptococci, clostridia, pathogens or other organisms.

# 6. SAMPLING

In the bacteriological examination of water supplies, samples may need to be taken from boreholes, wells, springs, rivers and impounding reservoirs; at different stages during water treatment; from the treated water leaving the works; and from points in the distribution system such as break-pressure tanks, service reservoirs, water towers, hydrants on mains, standpipes, specially provided sampling taps and consumers' premises. After disinfection of new and repaired mains, samples should be taken before the water is put into supply. New mains should not be put into service until satisfactory bacteriological results are obtained. In these situations, sampling procedures may vary considerably and for this reason staff should be specially trained for the work.

Ideally, samples from a supply should be taken at random but because of the complexity of distribution systems, this may not always be practicable. Sampling locations should therefore be so selected that an adequate assessment of water quality can be made. For this purpose, special sampling taps should be fitted by water undertakings at strategic points throughout the system. These primary sampling taps should not be used exclusively but as reference points where they will provide important information about certain districts, long pipe runs and dead ends. Routine samples should also be taken at random from consumers' taps to confirm that the hygienic quality of the water is satisfactory throughout the system. Samples should always be drawn from a tap connected to the main supply unless it is required to assess the bacteriological quality of the water contained in a storage cistern and the associated pipework. Storage cisterns are often inadequately covered, so that bacteriological contamination may occur through the introduction of dust, insects, birds, and small animals. In addition, exposure of stored water to light encourages the growth of algae.

## 6.1 The Collection, Storage and Transport of Samples for Bacteriological Examination

The prime objective is to obtain a sample which is representative as far as possible of the water to be examined. To achieve this, certain precautions are necessary which are common to all sampling procedures for the bacteriological examination of water:

— Sterile bacteriological sampling bottles must be used containing sodium thiosulphate to neutralize any chlorine in the water to be sampled,
— Scrupulous care should be taken to avoid accidental contamination of the sample during collection and subsequent handling,
— The changes which occur in the bacteriological content of water between the time of sampling and examination should be reduced to a minimum by ensuring that the sample is not exposed to light, is kept cool in an insulated container and is transported to the laboratory as quickly as possible,
— The sample should be examined as soon as possible after collection, preferably within six hours (PHLS, 1952, 1953 b).

Every sample bottle must be clearly identifiable, and the following information should be supplied with the sample:

| | |
|---|---|
| — Agency requesting the examination | Including address for correspondence **and** name and telephone number for direct contact. |
| — Sampled by: | |
| — Reference number: | |
| — Date and time of sampling: | |
| — Reason for sampling: | State whether routine, follow-up, complaint, mains' disinfection, etc. |
| — Supply: | Specify name of reservoir, treatment works, borehole, etc. |
| — Type of water: | State whether raw, treatment stage, final, distributed — and if so whether directly from mains or after storage. |

| | |
|---|---|
| — Location of sampling point: | Give address and location, such as kitchen tap, cistern tap, drinking fountain, storage tank, etc. |
| — Chlorine residual: | Free . . . . . . . . . . . . . mg/litre |
| | Total . . . . . . . . . . . mg/litre |

The following additional information may be helpful:
— The temperature of the water,
— Recent weather conditions,
— If from a well; its depth, construction, age and covering,
— If from a spring; whether the sample was taken from a collecting chamber,
— If from a river or stream; the depth at which the sample was taken, whether from the side or the middle of the stream and whether after spate, or during drought or normal conditions,
— If from a lake or reservoir; the position and depth of sampling,
— Observations on any possible sources of pollution in the vicinity and their distance from the sampling point,
— Any unusual feature or occurrence.

## 6.2 Technique of sampling

### 6.2.1 Sample bottles
Sterile bottles should be provided by the laboratory performing the examination and should be used exclusively for bacteriological purposes (see Appendix A).

### 6.2.2 Neutralization of Chlorine
As the water to be examined is likely to contain chlorine or chloramines, sufficient sodium thiosulphate must be added to sample bottles to neutralize these substances. For low concentrations of chlorine and at pH values normally occuring in water supply, sodium thiosulphate $(Na_2S_2O_3.5H_2O)$ at a concentration of 18 mg/litre should neutralize up to 5 mg/l of free and combined residual chlorine and has no significant effect on the coliform or *E. coli* content of unchlorinated water on storage (PHLS, 1953c). It is therefore recommended that at least this level of thiosulphate should be added to **all** bacteriological sample bottles before they are sterilized, the amount depending on the size of the bottle. Thus 0.1 ml of a 1.8 per cent (w/v) solution of sodium thiosulphate $(Na_2S_2O_3.5H_2O)$ should be added *pro rata* for each 100 ml of bottle capacity.

### 6.2.3 Order of taking Samples
When a number of samples for different purposes are to be taken from the same sampling point, certain precautions are necessary. The sample for bacteriological examination should be collected first unless special investigations are necessary, as, for example, to determine the cause of taste, odours or the concentration of metals in the first flush. For chlorine estimation, a bottle which does not contain thiosulphate should be used and, where possible, this test for chlorine should be done immediately on site.

28

To avoid contamination, samples for bacteriological examination should be kept strictly separate from all others. Boxes for the transport of samples should be made of materials that can be disinfected regularly. They should not be used for carrying anything other than samples of water for bacteriological examination.

### 6.2.4 Opening and filling of Sample Bottles
— Keep the sample bottle unopened until the moment it is required for filling.
— Never rinse out a bottle before taking a sample.
— Loosen the string or rubber band holding the cover in position; hold the bottle by the base in one hand and remove the stopper and cover together with the other hand.
— Retain the stopper and cover in the hand whilst the bottle is filled, and replace them immediately.
— Finally secure the cover.

### 6.2.5 Sampling from Taps
The necessity of flaming taps before taking samples — previously regarded as essential in order to obtain water representative of that in the distribution system — is open to question. It can be argued that flaming of tap outlets can have only a limited effect unless carried out to such an extent as to cause damage to the fittings. Moreover, any bacterial growth is more likely to occur on the washers, especially the inlet-side where flaming or disinfection is unlikely to be wholly effective. Provided that care is exercised over the choice of taps for sampling — which should be clean, free of all attachments and in good repair — and that the water is allowed to flow at a uniform rate for 2-3 minutes to establish equilibrium conditions, samples may be assumed to be acceptable for bacteriological examination. It should be noted that any alteration of the tap setting during sampling may have an adverse effect. For reasons of economy as well as good customer relations, it is therefore suggested that flaming taps is not necessary for routine samples from consumers' premises. If, however, there is any particular reason to doubt the effectiveness of this approach, then flaming or disinfection of the taps should be carried out.

### 6.2.5.1 ROUTINE SAMPLES
These should be taken from taps as follows:
— Do not use mixer taps. Remove all external fittings such as anti-splash devices or hoses,
— Remove grease and slime from the tap with a clean swab,
— Run the water to waste for at least 2-3 minutes in order to flush out the interior of the tap and service pipe,
— Fill the bottle from a gentle stream taking care to avoid splashing.

Occasionally, when a tap is turned on, water may leak slightly between the spindle and the gland. This is liable to run down the outside of the tap and, by gaining access to the sample, cause contamination. Under such conditions, no sample for bacteriological examination should be taken until the leak has been remedied.

## 6.2.5.2 SPECIAL SAMPLES

For primary sampling points, repeat samples and consumer complaints, it may be necessary to sterilize or disinfect the taps before the sample is taken as follows:

**Metal taps**
— Clean the tap and run the water to waste as above,
— Heat sterilize the tap, preferably with a blow torch,
— Run the water to waste again to cool the tap and fill the sample bottle as above.

**Plastic taps**
It is not possible to sterilize plastic taps *in situ* by heating as with metal taps. For this reason, the installation of metal sampling taps at selected locations as reference sampling points should be considered in areas where plastic taps predominate. Where it is necessary to take special samples from plastic taps, as for example after consumer complaints, the following procedure, despite its limitations, should be adopted:
— Run the water to waste for 2-3 minutes to clear the service pipe,
— Turn off the tap and clean the outer, and if possible the inner, surface of the mouth with a disposable swab soaked in a 1:10 solution of commercial hypochlorite (1 per cent available chlorine) and leave for 2-3 minutes,
— Run the water to waste for 5 minutes before taking the sample.

## 6.2.6 Sampling from Hydrants

Samples from public water supplies should preferably be taken from taps connected directly with the main. Where this is not possible, samples may be taken direct from the main by means of a hydrant. This is often necessary after the disinfection of a main when the water should be tested bacteriologically before the supply is brought into use. The procedure for sampling from a hydrant is as follows:
— If the hydrant box is full of water, bale out to below the frost plug of the hydrant bowl,
— Open the valve carefully to wash out debris from the hydrant bowl but do not flood the hydrant box,
— Bale out to at least 2.5 cm below the top of the hydrant bowl,
— Pour hypochlorite solution containing 5-10 per cent available chlorine into the hydrant bowl, taking care to avoid splashing of person or clothing,
— Screw on the stand post with the bibcock shut,
— Open the hydrant valve, then slowly open the bibcock. When the water charged with chlorine begins to run out, immediately close the bibcock,
— Wait for 5 minutes to allow the heavily chlorinated water to disinfect the standpost,
— Open the bibcock fully and allow the water to run to waste for at least 5 minutes, taking care that the hypochlorite-charged water does not splash clothing,
— Test for residual chlorine to ensure that all hypochlorite-charged water has been flushed to waste. If the chlorine residual is as expected

for the water in supply, adjust the bibcock to a gentle stream, and fill the sample bottle.

NOTE: Chlorine is highly toxic to fish, and the hypochlorite-charged water should not be allowed to run to waste to a water course.

### 6.2.7 Sampling from Service Reservoirs and Water Towers

Service reservoirs and water towers, because of their varied construction and locations, are particularly liable to contamination. For this reason, the quality of the outgoing water should be regularly monitored. Entry to these structures is sometimes difficult and there is always the attendant risk that accidental contamination may occur, for example, from the access cover or indeed from the footwear or clothing of the sampler. For routine purposes, it is therefore recommended that water samples should be taken preferably from specially fitted sampling taps. Alternatively, they may be obtained either by dipping or from the nearest property served by the supply.

### 6.2.8 Sampling from Surface Waters

The aim in collecting samples directly from a river, stream, lake, reservoir, spring or shallow well, must be to obtain samples representative of the water to be abstracted. It is therefore undesirable to take samples too near the bank, or too far from the point of draw-off. If abstraction is by means of a floating arm, the sample should not be taken from too great a depth. In streams or reservoirs, areas of relative stagnation should be avoided. Damage to the bank must be guarded against, otherwise fouling of the water may occur. Take the sample as follows:

— Remove the cover and stopper from the bottle and retain them in one hand,
— Hold the bottle by the base with the other hand and plunge it neck downwards below the surface to a depth of about 30cm,
— Tilt the bottle so that the neck points slightly upwards and point the mouth towards the current. Where no current exists, as in a reservoir, push the bottle forwards horizontally until full,
— Remove the bottle and replace the stopper immediately. Take care throughout that no water entering the bottle is likely to have come into previous contact with the hand.

If it is not possible to fill the bottle directly — as for example where there is a high bank — the sample may often be obtained from a bridge by lowering into the water a specially weighted sampling device, or a suitable container such as a metal jug. These may be sterilized either previously or on site. Alternatively, a long pole fitted with a clamp to hold the sampling bottle can be used.

### 6.2.9 Sampling from Wells

Where pumping is mechanical, the sample should be collected from a previously sterilized tap on the rising main before the water passes into a reservoir or cistern. If the well is fitted with a hand pump, clean and flame the mouth and operate the hand pump for at least 5 minutes before taking the sample. If the water is normally raised from the well by means of a pail or can, the sample should be collected by means of a sterile, weighted bottle or jug.

### 6.2.10 Sampling from Special Locations

When sampling from a deep well or borehole under construction, or from the depths of a lake or reservoir, a sterile, specially weighted bottle or other sampling device should be used. When sampling at different parts of a water treatment plant, not all of which are served by sampling taps, dip samples should be taken using either sterile, weighted sampling devices or a sample bottle attached to a long pole. It should be stressed that not all sampling taps in water treatment plants necessarily give a representative sample because of very long lengths of pipework. In these circumstances, it is advisable to run the water continuously to avoid stagnation and the possibility of microbial growth.

# 7. TECHNICAL METHODS

## 7.1 Introduction

In the following pages the various procedures for the bacteriological examination of water are set out in full. The purpose of this detailed description is not to prescribe a rigid set of rules from which any deviation is to be deprecated, but rather to specify techniques which are likely to be accompanied by little experimental error and to give reproducible results. It is left for the individual bacteriologist to decide whether any changes in technique will result in greater convenience or economy without appreciable loss in accuracy or in comparability with the results of other laboratories. It is important, however, that the reliability of the bacteriological techniques should be checked from time to time, both within laboratories and also between different laboratories by means of quality assessment procedures. For example, simulated water samples containing known organisms may be distributed periodically for examination (Barrow et al. 1978). Individual laboratories can also carry out replicate analyses on one or more routine samples on a regular basis, and statistical procedures can be applied to ascertain if these results are within acceptable limits (Eisenhart and Wilson, 1943).

The preparation and sterilization of the necessary glassware are described in Appendix A and methods for the preparation of media and reagents in Appendix B. These methods should be followed strictly if uniform results are to be obtained. For the same reason, the use of certain standard commercial preparations is occasionally recommended. The need for the regular monitoring of the performance and accuracy of laboratory equipment and for testing the quality of reagents and media is emphasized. Particular attention should be paid to the operating temperatures of incubators and water baths.

## 7.2 Laboratory Hygiene

In water examination, particular significance is attached to very small numbers of coliform organisms and E. coli. As these organisms are very common in man and his environment, and are cultivated routinely in the laboratory, special precautions are needed to avoid accidental contamination of the samples. The risk is greater in laboratories where faeces, sewage and other heavily contaminated materials are also examined. Wherever practicable a separate part of the laboratory should be set aside for the reception and examination of water samples. It should be secluded as far as possible from the passage of other workers and be free from draughts. Bench surfaces should be swabbed with disinfectant daily and immediately after accidental spillage. All cultures and used glassware, including containers and sample bottles, should be autoclaved before disposal or release for washing-up. All workers should wash their hands before starting examination of the samples and should preferably wear a clean laboratory coat or gown specially reserved for this purpose. Boxes or crates for the transport of samples should be made preferably of metal or plastics, so that they can be either autoclaved or disinfected at weekly intervals. They should be used solely for carrying samples of water for bacteriological examination and, to avoid contamination, they should not be placed on analytical benches.

## 7.3  Laboratory Safety

In the United Kingdom, the Health and Safety at Work legislation* places a clear duty on management with regard to safety in laboratories to ensure so far as is reasonably practicable the health, safety and welfare at work of all employees. Similarly, employers are enjoined not to expose the public to risks to their health and safety. Implementation of the Act is not solely a management responsibility, for safety continues to rest with the heads of the departments although they may delegate certain duties. Equally, individual employees have a duty to cooperate with their employers and take reasonable care for the health and safety, not only of themselves, but of their fellow workers and of the general public. In order to ensure that the requirements of the Act are being met, the Health and Safety Executive may inspect premises. The inspectorate also has the power to close laboratories and, in extreme instances, to take legal action.

Sound technique is the basis of safe microbiological procedures and it is important that all individuals concerned with this work should receive adequate training. It is also important that the necessary laboratory equipment and facilities should conform to accepted codes of safety and good practice (Collins, Hartley and Pilsworth, 1974; DHSS *et al* 1978; NWC, 1983).

## 7.4  Methods for the Detection and Enumeration of Indicator Organisms

As the number of indicator organisms in water may be very small, direct inoculation on solid media is not practicable and other methods must be used by which large volumes can be examined and by which the number of organisms in 100 ml of the sample can be estimated. Two procedures — the multiple-tube test, also known as the most probable number (MPN) or

---

*Health and Safety at Work etc. Act, 1974
Health and Safety at Work (Northern Ireland) Order, 1978

dilution method, and membrane filtration — are available. Both these techniques can be used to detect and enumerate each indicator organism, the media and incubation conditions differing according to the organism sought. Each method is therefore described in detail together with its application to the test for coliform organisms and *E. coli;* the variations necessary for the other indicator organisms are described in later sections. The preparation and dilution of the sample are the same for every test and these are described first.

## 7.5  Preparation of Samples

— Invert the sample-bottle rapidly several times in order to disperse any sediment.
— Remove the stopper or cap, and retain in the hand.
— Flame the mouth of the bottle, pour off some of the contents, replace the stopper or cap and again shake the bottle in order to distribute any organisms uniformly throughout the water.
— Make any dilutions required at this stage.

### 7.5.1  Diluent
— Use sterile quarter-strength Ringer's solution for all dilutions.

### 7.5.2  Making the Dilutions
— Measure out 90 or 9 ml of the diluent into sterile dilution bottles or tubes. Alternatively, use volumes of diluent pre-sterilized in screw-capped bottles.
— Make one or more ten-fold dilutions by transferring one volume of water sample to nine volumes of diluent.
— With a fresh pipette, mix thoroughly and carry over a similar volume to another nine volumes of diluent, and so on. Prepare enough of each dilution for all the tests to be carried out on the sample.

## 7.6  The Multiple Tube Method

### 7.6.1  Principle
In the multiple tube method of counting bacteria, measured volumes of water or of one or more dilutions are added to a series of tubes containing a liquid differential medium. It is assumed that on incubation each tube which received one or more test organisms in the inoculum will show growth and the characteristic change produced by the organism sought when growing in the medium used. Provided that negative results occur in some of the tubes, the most probable number of organisms in 100 ml of the sample can be estimated from the number and distribution of tubes showing a positive reaction. Confirmation that positive reactions are due to the growth of the specific indicator organism sought can be obtained by subculture to tubes of confirmatory media, some of which need to be incubated at a higher temperature. Positive reactions in the confirmatory tests yield further information about the types of organism present. The presumptive and confirmed counts are calculated by reference to probability tables.

## 7.6.2 Statistical Considerations

Various workers, of whom the first was McCrady (1915, 1918), have put forward formulae, based on the laws of probability, by means of which the numbers of organisms in 100 ml of water may be estimated when any given proportion of the inoculated tubes shows growth and other changes characteristic of the organism sought. The various mathematical approaches have been reviewed by Eisenhart and Wilson (1943), and Cochran (1950) has given an excellent introduction to the principles involved in the estimation of bacterial densities by dilution-methods. The tables given in Appendix C are based on those of Swaroop (1938; 1951), but give a greater number of combinations of positive and negative results, some of which in practice should occur only very rarely (Woodward, 1957; de Man, 1975).

The multiple tube method has a large "sampling error". For example, in the 11-tube test (1 x 50 ml, 5 x 10 ml, 5 x 1 ml) and for the 15-tube test (5 x 10 ml, 5 x 1 ml, 5 x 0.1 ml), the upper limit of the number of organisms likely to be present in the sample of water is about three times the MPN value and the lower limit between a third and a quarter of it. For any given estimation it is possible that the true figure lies beyond these limits, but this will occur in only about 5 per cent of all such estimations and therefore the upper limit can, for all practical purposes, be regarded as the maximum number of organisms the sample could contain. The calculations are based on the assumption that the organisms present in the water are evenly distributed and the importance of thoroughly mixing the sample cannot be stressed too strongly. Although the multiple tube method is very sensitive for the detection of small numbers of indicator organisms, the MPN is not a precise value. Apparent differences between results must therefore be interpreted with caution. It should be appreciated also that variation in bacterial numbers in the water source may be much greater than is indicated by the MPN range for a single sample.

## 7.6.3 Procedure

### 7.6.3.1 CHOICE OF VOLUMES FOR INOCULATION

— With waters expected to be of good quality, add one 50 ml volume and 5 x 10 ml volumes of the sample to equal volumes of double-strength medium.
— With waters of doubtful or unknown quality, use one 50 ml volume, 5 x 10 ml and 5 x 1 ml volumes; add the 1 ml volumes to 5 ml of single-strength medium.
— With more polluted waters include also 5 x 0.1 ml (5 x 1 ml of a 1 in 10 dilution) and omit the 50 ml volume of the sample.
— With heavily polluted waters, additional dilutions of 1 in 100, 1 in 1000 or higher, may be needed to give some negative reactions necessary for the MPN estimation.

### 7.6.3.2 INOCULATION OF THE CULTURE MEDIUM

— With a sterile straight-sided pipette or manual dispenser, add the 1 ml volumes of the water sample to tubes containing 5 ml of single-strength medium and the 10 ml volumes to tubes containing 10 ml of double-strength medium. Measure the 50 ml volume into a screw-capped bottle containing 50 ml of double-strength medium.

35

### 7.6.3.3 INCUBATION AND EXAMINATION OF THE CULTURES

— Incubate the inoculated tubes at the temperature specified, and examine them at set intervals, according to the indicator organism sought.
— Count the number of tubes of each volume showing a positive reaction and by reference to the Tables in Appendix C, calculate the most probable number of organisms present in 100 ml of the sample. For example, in a 15-tube test with 5 x 10 ml, 5 x 1 ml and 5 x 0.1 ml, if the number of tubes showing a positive reaction in each set of five tubes is 3 : 2 : 0, the MPN is 14 organisms per 100 ml.
— At this stage carry out any confirmatory tests that may be required.
— When using dilutions, choose a consecutive series of three ten-fold dilutions which show some positive and some negative reactions and multiply the MPN by the dilution factor according to the rules given in Appendix C.

## 7.7 The Count of Coliform Organisms and *Escherichia coli* by the Multiple Tube Method

### 7.7.1 Introduction
The test for coliform organisms and *E. coli* is the most important routine bacteriological examination carried out on drinking water, as it provides the most sensitive method for detecting faecal contamination.

### 7.7.2 Definitions
In the context of the method, coliform organisms ferment lactose within 48 hours at 37°C with the production of acid and gas. Thermotolerant coliform organisms show the same fermentative properties in 24 hours at 44°C. *E. coli* is a thermotolerant coliform organism which produces indole from tryptophan.

### 7.7.3 Principle
Isolation in a medium containing lactose, an indicator of acidity and an inner inverted (Durham) tube to detect gas formation.

### 7.7.4 Choice of Medium
Media may be made selective for the coliform group of organisms in two ways:
(a) An inhibitory substance may be added to suppress the growth of other organisms which may be present in the water. Traditionally, bile-salts have been used for this purpose as in MacConkey Broth. The composition of this medium is given for reference purposes only. More recently Teepol 610 has been used as a substitute for the natural, and therefore variable, bile-salts (Jameson and Emberley 1956). In other countries, sodium lauryl sulphate, one of the active ingredients of Teepol, has been used as in Lauryl Tryptose (Lactose) Broth (APHA 1976).
(b) Media may also be made selective by the use of chemically defined nutrients which can be utilized only by a limited number of bacterial species (Folpmers, 1948). The best of these is based on the Improved Formate Lactose Glutamate Medium described by Gray (1964). In all these media the

production of acid and gas is presumed to be due to the growth of coliform organisms.

In a comparative trial (PHLS/SCA 1980a), a minerals-modified variation of Gray's glutamate medium (PHLS, 1969) was compared with Lauryl Tryptose (Lactose) Broth (APHA, 1976). This showed that the glutamate medium was slightly superior, especially with chlorinated waters, and for samples with low counts (below about 50 per 100 ml) of coliform organisms and *E. coli*. The minerals-modified version of Gray's Improved Formate Lactose Glutamate Medium is therefore still recommended as the first choice for the enumeration of coliform organisms by the multiple tube method, even though some aerobic spore-bearing organisms may cause false-positive presumptive reactions on occasions. However, Lauryl Tryptose (Lactose) Broth, is an acceptable alternative.

### 7.7.5 Procedure

#### 7.7.5.1 INCUBATION AND EXAMINATION OF THE CULTURES
— After preparation of the sample, making any necessary dilutions and inoculating the tubes as described in 7.5 and 7.6.3 respectively, incubate them at 37° C and examine after 18-24 hours. Regard the presence of acid and gas in any tube as a positive reaction. At this stage, the gas may be visible as a bubble or may be seen only when the tube is tapped.
— Subculture each tube showing a positive reaction to tubes of confirmatory media (7.7.5.2). It is useful at this stage, especially in the examination of treated waters, to subculture to MacConkey Agar to obtain isolated colonies for further study.
— Reincubate the remaining tubes for a further 24 hours and sub-culture any more which show acid and gas formation.

Acid production with any amount of gas should be regarded as a positive result. This is generally true of all tubes examined after 24 hours, but when the gas is first seen at the 48-hour reading the acceptance of small amounts of gas may give, with some water-sources, too many false-positive results — reactions caused by organisms which cannot be confirmed as belonging to the coliform group. In such circumstances a positive result should be recorded only when sufficient gas has been produced to fill the concavity of the Durham tube. Some true positive results will however be missed if small amounts of gas are ignored (PHLS, 1968 a).

#### 7.7.5.2 CONFIRMATION AND DIFFERENTIATION OF COLIFORM ORGANISMS
The further investigation of positive reactions can be considered as two separate problems. First it is necessary to confirm that positive reactions are due to true coliform organisms; and secondly, a rapid and simple test is required to show whether *E. coli* is present or not. Further differentiation is rarely necessary, but may be useful in showing whether a given water is regularly contaminated by the same organism and hence in tracing the source of the pollution. The next step therefore is to confirm the presence of coliform organisms in each tube showing a positive presumptive reaction. With raw waters, confirmation and differentiation beyond the stage of thermotolerant

coliform organisms is rarely necessary. With chlorinated water, however, false positive tube-reactions may be caused by spore-bearing organisms which are more resistant to chlorination than coliform organisms and which are able to ferment lactose with the production of gas. With samples of chlorinated drinking water, it is therefore necessary to confirm the presumption that coliform organisms are present on every occasion. With pure cultures, Lactose Peptone Water is suitable for demonstrating gas production, but for subculture from positive presumptive reactions in tubes, confirmatory coliform media containing selective agents to inhibit the growth of spore bearing organisms are usually used, as for example, with Brilliant-green Lactose Bile Broth. Previously, Lactose Ricinoleate Broth was also used for this purpose but, because of its turbidity, gas production was sometimes difficult to see. Lauryl Tryptose Lactose Broth is therefore now recommended instead for the confirmation of both coliform and thermo-tolerant coliform organisms (PHLS/SCA, 1981). The procedure is as follows:
— Subculture each tube showing acid and gas in the multiple tube test to two tubes of either Brilliant-green Lactose Bile Broth or Lauryl Tryptose Lactose Broth (PHLS/SCA 1981),
— Incubate one tube at 37°C for 48 hours. Gas production within this time confirms the presence of coliform organisms,
— Incubate the other tube at 44°C for 24 hours. Gas production within this time confirms the presence of thermotolerant coliform organisms.

### 7.7.5.3  RAPID DETECTION OF E. coli
The rapid detection of E. coli depends partly on its ability to produce gas from lactose or mannitol at 44°C. Some other coliform organisms can also produce gas at this temperature, but few of them are able to produce indole at 44°C, which is characteristic of E. coli, and this provides a simple means of distinguishing between them.
— In addition to the tests carried out in 7.7.5.2, inoculate a tube of Tryptone Water, and incubate at 44°C for 24 hours.
— Add 0.2-0.3 ml of Kovacs' reagent. Indole formation (7.7.6.4) together with gas production from lactose at 44°C indicates the presence of E. coli.
  Although gas and indole formation can often be detected after incubation for only 6 hours, these tests should not be regarded as negative until after 24 hours' incubation (Taylor, 1955).
  With each batch of confirmatory and subsequent differential tests, two control tubes should be included, one inoculated with a known strain of E. coli and the other with a coliform organism such as Klebsiella aerogenes which does not produce gas from lactose at 44°C.

### 7.7.5.4  SINGLE-TUBE CONFIRMATORY TESTS FOR E. coli
Various workers have described media in which gas and indole formation can be demonstrated in a single tube (Schubert 1956; Fennell 1972; Pugsley, Evison and James 1973). In these media, mannitol is substituted for lactose. Lauryl Tryptose Mannitol Broth with Tryptophan added (PHLS/SCA 1980c) has also been found suitable for this purpose. Since single-tube media

may occasionally give false-negative results, it is essential if the indole reaction is negative that the test should be repeated in Tryptone Water by subculture from colonies on the MacConkey plate.

### 7.7.5.5 OXIDASE TEST

Some bacteria found in water may conform to the definition of coliform organisms in most respects, but are able to produce gas from lactose only at temperatures below 37°C. They therefore give negative results in the standard confirmatory tests for coliform organisms and their presence in water is not usually regarded as significant. Aeromonas species, which occur naturally in water, have an optimum growth temperature in the range 30-35°C but may nevertheless produce acid and gas from lactose at 37°C. They are of little sanitary significance and are distinguishable from the coliform group by a positive oxidase reaction. The oxidase test is carried out with pure cultures of lactose-fermenting organisms grown on Nutrient Agar medium as follows:

— Place 2-3 drops of freshly prepared Oxidase Reagent on a filter paper in a Petri dish,
— With a platinum (not nichrome) wire loop or glass rod, smear some of the growth on the prepared filter paper,
— Regard the appearance of a deep blue-purple colour within 10 seconds as a positive reaction.

It is desirable, on each occasion that the oxidase reagent is used, to conduct control tests with an organism known to give a positive reaction *(Ps. aeruginosa)* and one which gives a negative reaction *(E. coli).*


### 7.7.6 Further Differential Tests

### 7.7.6.1 CLASSIFICATION OF COLIFORM ORGANISMS

In routine water examination the exact identification of species by an extensive series of tests such as those described by Edwards and Ewing (1962) and Cowan (1974) is seldom necessary. It is usually sufficient, when any classification of strains is required, to apply the series of tests known collectively as IMViC (Wilson et al., 1935). These are the tests for indole formation, the methyl-red and Voges-Proskauer reactions, citrate utilization and the production of gas from lactose at 44°C. Thus, *E. coli* by this method would be recorded as $+ + - - 44 +$, *Klebsiella aerogenes* as $- - + + 44 -$, and the organism encountered in jute, formerly known as Irregular VI, would be designated $- - + + 44 +$. These relatively simple tests can be used to characterise most coliform organisms found in water without the use of specific names or the need to resort to one or other of the multitest differential identification systems now available.

### 7.7.6.2 SUBCULTURE FOR DIFFERENTIAL TESTS

On MacConkey Agar coliform colonies are usually circular in shape, convex or low-convex, with a smooth non-mucoid surface and entire edge. They are red, but the depth of colour varies considerably and colonial differences cannot be relied on for differentiation within the group.

— For further examination select and subculture two or three colonies, as far as possible of different appearance,

— Lightly touch each colony with a straight wire and make a suspension in a few drops of quarter-strength Ringer's solution in a small sterile tube. Use this bacterial suspension to inoculate the various media for the differential tests.

### 7.7.6.3 FERMENTATION OF LACTOSE

— Inoculate two tubes of Lactose Peptone Water and incubate one at 37°C for 48 hours. Acid and gas formation within this time confirms the presence of coliform organisms,

— Incubate the other tube at 44°C for 24 hours. The presence of any amount of gas after 6 to 24 hours' incubation confirms the presence of thermotolerant coliform organisms.

### 7.7.6.4 INDOLE TEST

— Inoculate a tube of Tryptone Water and incubate it at 37°C for 24 hours,

— Add 0.2-0.3 ml of Kovacs' reagent and shake the tube gently. A deep red colour developing almost immediately in the upper layer indicates a positive result.

### 7.7.6.5 METHYL-RED AND VOGES-PROSKAUER TESTS

— Inoculate a tube of Glucose Phosphate Medium and incubate for not less than two days at 37°C or three days at 30°C,

— Add two drops of 0.04 per cent methyl-red solution. A red colour indicates a positive reaction, a yellow colour a negative result. A pink or pale-red colour is best regarded as doubtful.

— Next add two drops of a 1 per cent (w/v) solution of creatine in 0.1 N HCl and, either 1 ml of a 40 per cent (w/v) solution, or a solid pellet of potassium hydroxide. Mix thoroughly, and observe for colour change. A pink colour denotes a positive reaction, no colour a negative reaction. As the colour is slow to develop, do not discard the tube as negative until four hours after the addition of the reagents.

### 7.7.6.6 CITRATE UTILISATION TEST

— Inoculate a tube of Koser's Citrate Medium by means of a straight wire dipped into the bacterial suspension (7.7.6.2),

— Incubate at 30°C and examine daily for growth for three days. To facilitate reading, bromothymol blue at a concentration of 0.008 per cent (w/v) may be added to the medium. Growth is accompanied by a colour change from pale green to bluish-green or blue. Simmon's Citrate Agar (1926) may be used instead.

## 7.8 The Membrane Filtration Method

### 7.8.1 Principle

In the membrane filtration method a measured volume of the water sample is filtered through a membrane composed of cellulose esters. The pore-size is such that the organisms to be enumerated are retained on or near the surface of the membrane which is then placed, normally face-upwards, on a differential medium selective for the indicator organism sought. This may be either an agar medium or an absorbent pad saturated with broth. On incubation at a specified temperature for a given time, it is assumed that the indicator organisms retained by the membrane will form colonies of characteristic morphology and colour depending on the medium used. The other organisms are either inhibited or can be distinguished by their colonial appearance. The colonies of the organism sought are counted and the result is expressed as the number per 100 ml of the sample.

## 7.8.2 Preparation and Sterilization of Equipment and Materials

### 7.8.2.1 FILTRATION APPARATUS
The membrane-filtration apparatus consists of a base supporting a porous disc. The filter funnel, which should be graduated at 50 ml and 100 ml, is secured to the base by means of screw-threads, clamps or by magnetic action. The filtration apparatus is usually connected to a vacuum source. For the examination of large numbers of water samples, multiple filtration units may be used. Each day, the filtration apparatus, including spare funnels and funnel stands, should be sterilized in the autoclave. At lease three funnels are required for one apparatus so that one funnel can be disinfected by immersion in boiling distilled water for at least one minute between samples. After disinfection, each funnel should be placed in a stand and allowed to cool before use.

### 7.8.2.2 MEMBRANES
Membrane filters, 47 mm in diameter, with a rated nominal pore-size of 0.45 µm or membranes which have similar filtration characteristics, are recommended; these will retain satisfactorily all the bacteria mentioned in this Report. The use of membranes with grid-marks is recommended to facilitate counting. It is necessary to check periodically that the membranes used are suitable for the organisms sought in the waters examined. Quality control assurance is important and membranes must be free from toxic substances. When membranes with grid-marks are used, bacterial growth should not be inhibited or stimulated along the lines.

Membranes are available pre-sterilized or they can be sterilized in the laboratory either by autoclaving at 115° C for 10 minutes or by boiling gently in distilled water for 10 minutes before use. It is important to note that the filtration properties of membranes are readily impaired by overheating, so that careful autoclave control is required.

### 7.8.2.3 RE-USE OF MEMBRANES IN EMERGENCY SITUATIONS
Ideally, membranes should be used only once. If necessary, they may be reused in emergency situations though only for *E. coli* and other coliform organisms, as follows:
— Select membranes with little or no growth, and place them in boiling water for one minute,
— Wash them gently in running water for several hours,
— Screen the membranes in bright light for any evidence of damage,
— Remove damaged membranes and immerse the remainder in 3 per cent (v/v) hydrochloric acid,

— Bring the acid to the boil and then pour off immediately,
— Wash the membranes at least three times in sterile distilled water,
— For the final rinse, add a trace of bromocresol purple and sufficient sodium bicarbonate to neutralize any remaining acid and bring the water to the boil. The membranes are then ready for re-use,
— If the membranes are not required immediately, bring the water to the boil again just before use.

## 7.8.2.4 ABSORBENT PADS

Absorbent pads of at least the same diameter as the membranes and approximately 1 mm thick should be used. They should be made of high quality paper fibres, uniformly absorbent and free from any toxic substances which could inhibit bacterial growth. Absorbent pads are available pre-sterilized or they can be sterilized in the autoclave in bundles of 50 to 100, preferably at 121°C for 20 minutes either in containers or wrapped in waterproof paper or foil.

— Place each individual pad with aseptic precautions in a sterile Petri dish or similar container.

## 7.8.2.5 MEDIA

The details of the media recommended are given in Appendix B. The media used with membrane filters differ in composition from those for the Multiple Tube method because membranes selectively adsorb some substances but not others; there is also a differential adsorbent capacity between the nutrient pad and the membrane. Dehydrated media should be reconstituted according to the manufacturers' instructions. Alternatively, the media may be prepared in the laboratory from approved high quality constituents. Sterile broth is dispensed aseptically onto each filter pad in sterile Petri dishes or similar containers: this may be done conveniently with an automatic pipette. The pad should be completely saturated with broth. When agar medium is used the surface of the agar should be completely smooth and dry.

## 7.8.2.6 INCUBATORS AND WATER BATHS

Accurate temperature control of incubators is essential. When resuscitation techniques involving pre-incubation at a lower temperature are required, manual transfer between different incubators can be avoided if one with fan-assisted air circulation and fitted with a time control to give automatic switching between the two temperatures is used. Incubators of this type function adequately only when the lower temperature is at least 5°C above ambient. When incubators are required to operate in an environment where the ambient temperature may approach within 5°C of the lower temperature, the use of a cooled incubator is recommended. Instead of incubators, dual time-temperature controlled water baths with circulation may be used. With water baths, it is essential to use suitable water-tight immersible containers to hold the Petri dishes.

## 7.8.3 Procedure

### 7.8.3.1 PREPARATION OF SAMPLES

The volumes should be chosen so that the number of colonies to be counted on the membrane lies, if possible, between 10 and 100. With some waters, it may be advantageous to filter different volumes so that the number of colonies on one of the membranes is likely to fall within this range. For treated waters filter 100 ml of the sample; for polluted waters either filter smaller volumes or dilute the sample before filtration. When the volume to be filtered is less than 10 ml, add at least 20 ml of sterile diluent to the funnel before addition of the sample to aid uniform dispersion of the bacteria over the entire surface of the membrane during filtration.

### 7.8.3.2  FILTRATION PROCEDURE

— Place the sterile filtration apparatus in position and connect to a source of vacuum,
— Remove the funnel and place a sterile membrane, grid-side upwards, on the porous disc of the filter base. Grasp only the outer part of the membrane filter with flat-ended sterile forceps,
— Replace the sterile funnel securely on the filter base,
— With the vacuum stopcock turned off, pour or pipette the required volume of water sample into the funnel,
— Open the stopcock and apply a vacuum of about 500 mm of mercury to filter the water slowly through the membrane,
— Close the stopcock as soon as the sample has been filtered so that as little air as possible is drawn through the membrane,
— Remove the funnel and transfer the membrane carefully either to a pad saturated with the medium or to a well-dried agar plate. Ensure that no air-bubbles are trapped between the membrane and the medium,
— Pour of any excess medium from the saturated pad, either before or after the membrane is placed in position. If this is not done, confluent growth may result,
— For different volumes of the same sample, the funnel may be re-used without boiling provided that the smallest volumes are filtered first,
— For different samples, remove a funnel from the boiling water bath, allow to cool and repeat the filtration process,
— After filtration of each sample, disinfect the funnel by immersion in boiling distilled water for at least one minute. During the filtration of a series of samples the filter base need not be disinfected unless it is contaminated or a membrane is damaged,
— Do not alternate the filtration of known polluted samples with those of treated water samples through the same apparatus,
— Filter all the samples of chlorinated water and those expected to give negative results first, and then those known to be polluted. Alternatively, a separate membrane filtration apparatus can be reserved for all chlorinated samples and another for polluted samples.

### 7.8.3.3  INCUBATION AND EXAMINATION

— Place the Petri dishes with the membranes inside a container with a tightly-fitting lid to prevent drying out. Alternatively, a polythene bag may be used and carefully folded over, tied or sealed. For anaerobic organisms, special incubation conditions are required.

- Incubate the membranes at the temperature and for the time specified for the organism sought.
- After incubation, count the characteristic colonies on the membrane in good light, if necessary with a hand lens. As colours are liable to change on cooling and standing, count the colonies within a few minutes of removal from the incubator or water bath.
- Express the result as the number of the indicator organism per 100 ml of water sample.

### 7.8.4 Statistical Considerations

Counts on membranes are subject to statistical variation and replicate tests on the same sample of water are unlikely to give the same number of colonies. If the organisms are randomly dispersed in the sample then this variation will be Poisson in distribution. For a colony count (C), the 95 per cent confidence limits for the numbers of organisms likely to be present in 100 ml of the water sample are given by the following approximate formula derived from Haight (1967):

$$C + 2 \pm 2 \sqrt{C+1}$$

For example, if 100 colonies are present on the membrane, then the actual number of the particular organism in 100 ml of the water sample is likely to lie between 82 and 122. However, for low counts of less than about 20 colonies, this approximate formula becomes inaccurate — as do all others; reference should then be made to Poisson tables, such as those in Geigy (1970) — from which the following examples are taken.

| Membrane colony count | 95 per cent confidence limits | |
|---|---|---|
| | Lower | Upper |
| 1 | 0 | 4 |
| 5 | 0 | 11 |
| 10 | 3 | 18 |
| 15 | 7 | 24 |
| 20 | 11 | 30 |

### 7.8.5 Advantages and Limitations of the Membrane Filtration Method

#### 7.8.5.1 ADVANTAGES

The outstanding advantage of the membrane filtration technique is the speed with which results can be obtained as direct counts. For example, presumptive coliform and *E. coli* counts may be available within 18 hours. This enables more rapid corrective action to be taken when required and allows a supply or equipment to be put back into service more quickly when a satisfactory result is obtained.

In the laboratory, there is considerable saving in technical labour and in the amount of media and glassware required,

The conditions of incubation can be varied easily to encourage the growth

44

of attenuated or slow-growing organisms,

False-positive reactions that may occur with some media in the multiple-tube test for coliform organisms due to the growth of aerobic or anaerobic spore-bearing organisms, or to mixtures of organisms, are unlikely to occur with membranes.

### 7.8.5.2 LIMITATIONS

In the membrane filtration method, gas production — for example by coliform organisms — is not detected,

Membranes are unsuitable for use with waters of high turbidity containing small numbers of the indicator organism sought. In these circumstances the membrane will become blocked before sufficient water can be filtered,

The membrane method is also unsuitable for water containing only small numbers of the indicator organism sought in the presence of many other bacteria capable of growth on the medium used.

## 7.9 The Count of Coliform Organisms and *Escherichia coli* by the Membrane Filtration Method

### 7.9.1 Principle

Isolation of the organisms on a membrane placed on an absorbent pad saturated with broth containing lactose and phenol red as an indicator of acidity, with subsequent confirmation of the ability to produce gas and, where necessary, indole formation.

### 7.9.2 Definitions

In the context of the method, organisms which produce acid from lactose and form yellow colonies on membranes after incubation for 4 hours at 30°C, followed by 14 hours at 37°C are regarded as presumptive coliform organisms. Similarly, organisms which produce acid from lactose after incubation for 4 hours at 30°C followed by 14 hours at 44°C, are presumed to be thermotolerant coliform organisms.* *E. coli* is a thermotolerant coliform organism which produces gas from lactose (or mannitol) and which also produces indole from tryptophan.

### 7.9.3 Choice of medium

Membrane Enriched Broth containing 0.4 per cent (v/v) Teepol 610 was previously recommended in the United Kingdom for the enumeration of coliform organisms and *E. coli* in water (DHSS *et al.*, 1969). However, because this particular blend of surfactant was not then available, a multi-laboratory trial was carried out to find a suitable alternative (PHLS/SCA 1980b). Sodium lauryl sulphate (0.1 per cent w/v) was found to be satisfactory and is now recommended in Membrane Lauryl Sulphate Broth. If stocks of Teepol 610 are still available, Membrane Enriched Teepol Broth may, however, still be used.

---

*"Thermotolerant coliform organisms" are equivalent to "faecal coliforms" specified in Water Directives of the European Community.

45

### 7.9.4 Procedure

#### 7.9.4.1 INCUBATION AND EXAMINATION OF MEMBRANES FOR COLIFORM ORGANISMS
— After preparation and filtration of the sample as described in 7.8.3, incubate the membranes for 4 hours at 30° C, and then for 14 hours at 37° C ± 0.5° C,
— Examine the membranes under good light, if necessary with a hand lens. Count all yellow colonies irrespective of size; do this within a few minutes of removal from the incubator as colours are liable to change on cooling and standing. Ignore pink or colourless colonies unless they are excessive in number when they may interfere with the growth of coliform organisms.

#### 7.9.4.2 INCUBATION AND EXAMINATION OF MEMBRANES FOR THERMOTOLERANT COLIFORM ORGANISMS AND *E. coli*
— Incubate the membranes for 4 hours at 30° C, and then for 14 hours at 44° C ± 0.25° C,
— Count the yellow colonies within a few minutes of removal from the water bath or incubator. Provided that the membranes are not overcrowded, colonies of *E. coli* usually have a characteristic appearance: bright yellow in colour and more than 1 mm in diameter.

A total incubation period of 18 hours is recommended for the enumeration of coliform organisms and *E. coli*. If however, a result is required urgently the membranes may be examined after 12 hours and if no colonies of any kind are present, a nil count can be assumed, but the membranes should be returned to the incubator for the full period of 18 hours.

It is important to note that the counts of yellow colonies at 37° C and at 44° C are only presumptive results. For the examination of raw or partly-treated waters, this is usually sufficient, but for potable supplies, whether treated or not, it is essential to carry out confirmatory tests for coliform organisms and *E. coli* to assess the sanitary significance of the results. In operational practice any positive result must be notified immediately so that corrective action can be taken. However, it must be appreciated that, since gas production is not detected in the membrane filtration method, there is an additional presumption that the organisms forming yellow, acid colonies can also produce gas. This is liable to lead to an overestimate of the number of coliform organisms but the error is on the side of safety and moreover, the result is available in a shorter time than by the multiple tube method.

#### 7.9.4.3 CONFIRMATION AND DIFFERENTIATION OF COLIFORM ORGANISMS
— Subculture all yellow colonies, or a representative number of them, to tubes of Lactose Peptone Water containing an inner inverted (Durham) tube to detect gas formation. As an alternative to Lactose Peptone Water, use a single-tube confirmatory medium as described in 7.7.5.4,
— Incubate these tubes at 37° C and examine them for the presence of acid and gas after 24 hours and, if the results are negative, after a further 24 hours,
— It is advantageous to subculture after about 6 hours' incubation

from the Lactose Peptone Water to plates of Nutrient Agar and MacConkey Agar to check for purity and colonial appearance,
— Carry out the oxidase test on colonies from the Nutrient Agar plate as described in 7.7.5.5.

Yellow colonies on membranes incubated at 37°C are confirmed as coliform organisms if both acid and gas are produced in Lactose Peptone Water, and if the oxidase test is negative. Since some species of Aeromonas also produce acid, and sometimes gas, from lactose, the oxidase test is essential for excluding them. Although certain tests, such as those for oxidase and indole, can be performed directly on colonies on membranes, the results may be doubtful and subculture of the colonies is not always satisfactory afterwards. Any subculture necessary should therefore be made before the application of any test reagents to colonies on membrane filters.

Coliform organisms may be classified further by the IMViC series of tests as described in 7.7.6.

### 7.9.4.4  CONFIRMATION OF *E. coli*
— Subculture all yellow colonies, or a representative number of them, to tubes of Lactose Peptone Water and tubes of Tryptone Water.
— Incubate them at 44°C for 24 hours and examine the tubes of Lactose Peptone Water for the presence of acid and gas.
— Add 0.2—0.3 ml of Kovacs' reagent to the tubes of Tryptone Water. Development of a red colour indicates the production of indole.
— As an alternative to separate tubes of Lactose Peptone Water and Tryptone Water, subculture yellow colonies to a single-tube confirmatory medium, as described in 7.7.5.4.

Yellow colonies on membranes incubated at 44°C are regarded as *E. coli* if acid and gas are produced in Lactose Peptone Water and the indole test is positive. At this stage, subcultures may be made from the Lactose Peptone Water to Nutrient Agar for the oxidase reaction, although as aeromonads rarely grow at 44°C, this test is not usually done. As a routine procedure, it is not always necessary to carry out further tests for the differentiation of *E. coli* but if required, the Methyl-red and Voges-Proskauer tests as described in 7.7.6.5 and the citrate utilisation test described in 7.7.6.6. — or alternatively one of the multi-test identification systems — may be used.

When yellow oxidase-negative colonies subcultured from the membrane incubated at 44°C cannot be confirmed as *E. coli,* further tests should be carried out as described in 7.9.4.3. to confirm that they are in fact coliform organisms.

### 7.9.4.5  MEMBRANE TRANSPORT MEDIUM
Ideally, water samples should be dispatched to the laboratory and examined with the minimum of delay, preferably within six hours of collection. If for any reason this presents difficulties, the samples of water may be filtered on site through membranes which are then placed on absorbent pads saturated with a transport medium such as that of Panezai, Macklin and Coles (1965). This is a very dilute medium on which coliform organisms survive but do not develop into visible colonies within three days when kept at ambient temperature. For despatch to the laboratory, small polystyrene dishes are recommended. On arrival, the membranes are transferred directly to

absorbent pads saturated with growth medium for incubation.

## 7.10  The Test For Faecal Streptococci

### 7.10.1  Introduction
In the United Kingdom streptococci are regarded as secondary indicators of faecal pollution, and the main use of the faecal streptococcus test is to assess the significance of coliform organisms in a sample of water in the absence of *E. coli*. Occasionally, identification of the species of streptococci present may help to distinguish between human and animal pollution.

### 7.10.2  Definitions
In the context of the methods, faecal streptococci are Gram-positive cocci which form pairs or chains and possess Lancefield's Group D antigen. They can grow in the presence of bile salts; in concentrations of sodium azide inhibitory to coliform organisms and most other Gram-negative bacteria; and at a temperature of 45°C. They also hydrolyse aesculin and are catalase-negative. Some species resist heating at 60°C for 30 minutes, grow in nutrient broth containing 6.5 per cent sodium chloride, and at pH 9.6.

    *Str. faecalis* and some related species reduce 2,3,5-triphenyl-tetrazolium chloride (TTC) to the insoluble red dye — formazan. Other species reduce TTC weakly or not at all.

### 7.10.3  Toxicity of Sodium Azide
Many of the media described in this section contain sodium azide. As this substance is highly toxic, great care should be taken in preparing these media especially when dehydrated ingredients in powder form are used. Sodium azide also has the property of forming explosive compounds with metals, especially copper. Waste material containing sodium azide must therefore be discarded with care, preferably through plastic pipes. Azide compounds may be decomposed and rendered safe by an excess of sodium nitrite.

### 7.10.4  The Count of Faecal Streptococci by the Multiple Tube Method

#### 7.10.4.1  PRINCIPLE
Culture of the sample in a liquid enrichment medium containing sodium azide, glucose and bromcresol purple as indicator. Growth and acid production indicate a positive result and therefore the presumptive presence of faecal streptococci. Subculture to confirmatory media to demonstrate growth at 44-45°C and hydrolysis of aesculin.

#### 7.10.4.2  CHOICE OF MEDIUM
Glucose Azide Broth (Hannay and Norton, 1947) is recommended as the liquid enrichment medium.

#### 7.10.4.3  PROCEDURE
##### 7.10.4.3.1  Incubation and Examination of the Cultures
— After preparation of the sample and making any necessary dilutions as described in 7.5, inoculate the test volumes into tubes of single or

double strength Glucose Azide Broth as described in 7.6.3,
— Incubate the tubes at 37°C and examine them after 24 and 48 hours for growth and acid production. At the 48 hour reading regard any trace of acidity as a positive reaction.

### 7.10.4.3.2 Confirmatory Tests
Two methods may be used to confirm the presence of faecal streptococci:

**Either** — Transfer a heavy inoculum from each tube showing a positive reaction to fresh tubes of Glucose Azide Broth and incubate at 44-45°C for 48 hours. Growth and acid formation at this temperature indicate the presence of faecal streptococci. In this method some false-positive reactions may be given by other Gram-positive organisms which can grow at this temperature.

**Or** — Alternatively, from each tube giving a positive reaction, place one drop or loopful of the growth on the surface of a plate of Bile Aesculin Azide Agar and incubate at 44-45°C. Development of a black or brown colour in or around the inoculum within a few hours confirms the presence of faecal streptococci. If the inocula are well spaced out, many cultures can be tested on one plate.

— From the number of tubes giving a positive confirmatory reaction, calculate the most probable number of faecal streptococci in 100 ml of the sample by reference to the Tables in Appendix C.

The Catalase test is used to distinguish streptococci, which are catalase-negative, from other Gram-positive cocci. Since this test can only be done with pure cultures, its application in the MPN method requires subculture to solid media.

## 7.10.5 The Count of Faecal Streptococci by the Membrane Filtration Method

### 7.10.5.1 PRINCIPLE
Filtration of a volume of the sample through a membrane, incubation on an agar medium containing sodium azide and TTC, and a count of all red, maroon or pink colonies that develop. Subculture to confirmatory media to demonstrate growth and the fermentation of glucose at 44-45°C or the hydrolysis of aesculin.

### 7.10.5.2 CHOICE OF MEDIUM
The glucose azide medium of Slanetz and Bartley (1957), referred to as Membrane Enterococcus Agar, is recommended. For confirmation, the media described in 7.10.4.3.2 should be used.

### 7.10.5.3 PROCEDURE
#### 7.10.5.3.1 Incubation and Examination of the Cultures
— After preparation of the sample and making any necessary dilutions as described in 7.5, filter the test volumes as described in 7.8.3 and place each membrane on the surface of a well-dried plate of Membrane Enterococcus Agar.
— Incubate **either** at 37°C for 48 hours **or** at 37°C for 4 hours and then at

49

44-45°C for a further 44 hours.

— Count all red, maroon or pink colonies as presumptive faecal streptococci. As not all species reduce TTC, pale colonies should not be ignored, especially when maroon or pink colonies are absent or present in only small numbers.

Although incubation throughout at 37°C may yield a higher count, it allows some organisms to grow which do not conform to the definition of faecal streptococci and cannot be confirmed as such. Incubation at 44-45°C thus has a selective effect and produces fewer false-positive results. The preliminary incubation at 37°C encourages the recovery of stressed organisms. In addition, some strains temporarily lose their ability to grow at 45°C outside the body (Allen, Pierce and Smith, 1953). If no confirmatory tests are done, the number of red or pink colonies growing on the membrane may be taken as a presumptive or unconfirmed count. The scope of the examination depends on the type of water being examined and the information required.

### 7.10.5.3.2  Confirmatory tests

— Use one of the methods described in 7.10.4.3.2. Subculture to Bile Aesculin Azide Agar gives a more rapid result and is therfore preferable. In addition, with colonies from membranes, the catalase test (7.10.6.1) may be performed directly.

## 7.10.6  Additional Confirmatory and Differential Tests

Although the possession of Lancefield's Group D antigen is referred to in the definition, serological methods of confirmation present many practical difficulties and their use is therefore not recommended in routine water examination.

Tolerance of 40 per cent bile is also characteristic of faecal streptococci, but in practice this test is not usually necessary and growth on MacConkey Agar can be used instead. Further tests with subcultures may be done if necessary, partly as an aid to species differentation. However, full identification depends on the demonstration of biochemical and other characteristics as described by Cowan (1974) or by means of one of the multi-test differential systems now available. *Str. faecalis* may be identified as described in 7.10.6.6.

### 7.10.6.1  CATALASE TEST

— Emulsify some of the culture to be tested in a few drops of quarter-strength Ringer's solution in a small screw-capped bottle. Add a drop of 3 per cent hydrogen peroxide solution and replace the cap. The appearance of bubbles (of oxygen) indicates catalase activity. Alternatively add the hydrogen peroxide to an overnight culture of the organism in a tube of either Nutrient Agar or Nutrient Broth.

The test should preferably not be performed on a slide because of the risk of aerosol formation.

### 7.10.6.2  BILE TOLERANCE

— Subculture to a plate or tube of Bile Agar (40 per cent) and incubate at 37°C for 24-48 hours. Growth on this medium indicates bile tolerance,
— Alternatively, use MacConkey Agar to show growth in the presence of

bile salts. Faecal streptococci form small deep red colonies on this medium.

### 7.10.6.3 HEAT RESISTANCE
— Transfer 1 ml of a 24 hour broth culture to a small test tube, and place it in a water bath at 60°C for 30 minutes. Cool the tube rapidly and incubate at 37°C for 24 hours. Subculture to a Blood Agar plate or other non-selective medium, incubate and examine for growth.

### 7.10.6.4 GROWTH AT pH 9.6
— Inoculate a tube of Glucose Phenolphthalein Broth (Clarke, 1953) and incubate at 37°C for 24 hours. Tolerance of pH 9.6 is indicated by heavy growth and decolourization of the medium.

### 7.10.6.5 SALT TOLERANCE
— Inoculate a tube of Nutrient Broth containing 6.5 per cent of sodium chloride (Salt Broth) and incubate at 37°C for 24-48 hours. Examine for growth.

### 7.10.6.6 IDENTIFICATION OF *Streptococcus faecalis*
*Str. faecalis* is particularly associated with man (Mead, 1964, 1966) and its presence thus suggests that pollution is of human origin, although its absence does not exclude this possibility.
— Subculture suspected colonies onto Tyrosine Sorbitol Thallous Acetate Agar (Mead 1963, 1964), and incubate at 44-45°C for 3 days. Differentiation depends on the ability of *Str. faecalis* to reduce TTC at pH 6.2, to ferment sorbitol, produce tyrosine decarboxylase and to grow at 45°C in the presence of 0.1 per cent (w/v) thallous acetate. The colonies on this medium have a uniform deep maroon colour and are encircled by a clear zone where the tyrosine has been decomposed.

## 7.11 The Test for Sulphite-reducing Clostridia and *Clostridium perfringens*

### 7.11.1 Introduction
The tests for sulphite-reducing clostridia play only a subsidiary role in water examination. These organisms form spores which are resistant to heating compared with vegetative cells and advantage is taken of this for the detection of clostridia in water. *Cl. perfringens,* an important member of this group, is associated with faecal contamination; if it is found at a time when other faecal indicator organisms are no longer detectable, it indicates remote or intermittent pollution.

### 7.11.2 Definitions
In the context of the methods, sulphite-reducing clostridia are Gram-positive, anaerobic spore-forming rods which reduce sulphites to sulphides. *Cl. perfringens* forms a stormy clot in Litmus Milk Medium.

### 7.11.3 The Count of Sulphite-reducing Clostridia and *Clostridium perfringens* by the Multiple Tube Method

### 7.11.3.1 PRINCIPLE
After preliminary heat treatment to destroy vegetative bacteria, culture of test

volumes of the sample in bottles of a liquid medium containing sodium sulphite and ferric citrate. Subculture of all bottles showing blackening to a confirmatory medium.

### 7.11.3.2  CHOICE OF MEDIUM
Differential Reinforced Clostridial Medium (Gibbs and Freame 1965) is recommended for isolation. It should be distributed in screw-capped bottles instead of tubes, with sufficient depth of medium to ensure adequate anaerobiosis during incubation. Litmus Milk is recommended as the confirmatory medium.

### 7.11.3.3  PROCEDURE
#### 7.11.3.3.1  Preparation of the Sample
— Heat the sample to 75°C in a water bath and maintain it at this temperature for 10 minutes. The time needed to reach this temperature can be determined with a similar bottle containing the same volume of water and a thermometer.
— After heat treatment, make any dilutions necessary as described in 7.5.

#### 7.11.3.3.2  Inoculation of the Medium
— Add the 50 ml and 10 ml test volumes to equal volumes of double-strength medium in screw-capped bottles and the 1 ml volumes to 25 ml of single-strength medium in 1 oz (28 ml) universal containers,
— Top-up with single-strength medium so as to leave a minimum amount of air space,
— A considerable amount of gas may be produced in this test and for the 50 ml volumes in particular, the use of a stout glass or plastic bottle is advisable. These should be placed inside a plastic bag to contain any breakage or spillage during incubation.

#### 7.11.3.3.3  Incubation and examination of the cultures
— Incubate the bottles at 37°C for 48 hours. A positive reaction is shown by blackening of the medium caused by reduction of sulphite and the precipitation of ferrous sulphide. A count made at this stage represents the number of spores of sulphite-reducing clostridia.

#### 7.11.3.3.4  Confirmation of *Cl. perfringens*
— Transfer a loopful from each bottle showing a positive reaction to a tube of Litmus Milk Medium which has been freshly steamed to expel the dissolved oxygen and cooled. Growth is improved in the litmus milk by adding to each tube a nail or a short length of iron wire sterilized by heating to redness immediately before inoculation.
— Incubate at 37°C for 48 hours. The tubes containing *Cl. perfringens* will show a "stormy clot" reaction, in which, as a result of lactose fermentation, the milk is acidified and coagulated, and the clot is disrupted by gas and often blown up the tube.
— From the number of tubes showing a positive reaction, calculate the most probable number of *Cl. perfringens* spores in 100 ml of the sample by reference to the Tables in Appendix C.

### 7.11.4 The Count of Sulphite-reducing Clostridia and *Clostridium perfringens* by the Membrane Filtration Method

**7.11.4.1 PRINCIPLE**

After preliminary heat treatment to destroy vegetative bacteria, filtration of a volume of the sample through a membrane, incubation anaerobically with a sulphite-containing agar medium, and a count of all black colonies that develop. Subculture to a confirmatory medium to demonstrate the presence of *Cl. perfringens*.

**7.11.4.2 CHOICE OF MEDIUM**

Several variations of sulphite-containing media and culture methods for anaerobic growth are available for the detection of sulphite-reducing clostridia. Membrane Clostridial Agar, a modification of the medium and method described by Burman, Oliver and Stevens (1969), is recommended. Whilst this method may give good reproducibility, it may be less sensitive than the multiple tube method with Differential Reinforced Clostridial Medium. Litmus Milk is used for confirmation of the presence of *Cl. perfringens*.

**7.11.4.3 PROCEDURE**

**7.11.4.3.1 Incubation and Examination of the Cultures**

— After heating the sample as described in 7.11.3.3.1, and making any necessary dilutions as in 7.5, filter the test volume as described in 7.8.3.

**Either** — Place each membrane face-upwards on the base of a sterile small (50 mm) Petri dish. Make sure that no air bubbles are trapped between the membrane filter and the bottom of the Petri dish,

— Pour carefully 18 ml of molten Membrane Clostridial Agar at 50° C over the membrane and allow it to set. Ensure that the membrane remains well below the surface of the agar medium,

— Invert the Petri dish and incubate aerobically at 37° C,

**Or** — Place each membrane face-upwards on the surface of a well-dried plate of Membrane Clostridial Agar,

— Incubate the Petri dishes without inversion in an anaerobic jar at 37° C,

— Examine the plates after 24 and 48 hours and count all black colonies as sulphite-reducing colstridia.

**7.11.4.3.2 Confirmation of *Cl. perfringens***

— Using a straight wire, subculture each colony to be tested into a tube or bottle of freshly steamed and cooled Litmus Milk Medium. Proceed as in 7.11.3.3.4,

— Regard a stormy clot reaction in Litmus Milk Medium as confirmation of *Cl. perfringens*.

## 7.12 The Colony Count

### 7.12.1 Introduction
In the United Kingdom the usual method of counting heterotrophic bacteria in water is by the pour-plate method with Yeast-Extract Agar. Separate counts are made of those aerobic mesophilic organisms which form visible colonies in this medium after 24 hours incubation at 37° C, and of those which form colonies after 3 days at 20-22° C. The two methods give different results, the interpretation of which is discussed in Section 3.2.1. The most useful application of the colony count is to detect change, especially sudden change, in the bacterial content of certain waters. It is therefore important that the same technique should always be used to examine a given water and that the method and medium employed should be stated in the report.

### 7.12.2 Definition
In the context of the method, the colonies comprise bacteria, yeasts and moulds capable of growth under the conditions specified.

### 7.12.3 The Colony Count by the Pour-Plate Method
#### 7.12.3.1 PRINCIPLE
Mixing of test volumes of the water sample with molten Yeast-Extract Agar in Petri dishes, incubation under the conditions specified, and a count of the colonies that develop.

#### 7.12.3.2 PROCEDURE
##### 7.12.3.2.1 Preparation of the Sample
— Prepare the samples as described in 7.5. Use the sample neat, or make one, two or more tenfold dilutions of it according to the bacterial content expected,
— Measure 1 ml volumes from the highest dilution into each of two Petri dishes and, using the same pipette, from the other dilutions and finally from the undiluted sample into each of four separate Petri dishes,
— Pour 15 ml of Yeast-Extract Agar, previously melted and cooled to 45-50°C, into each dish,
— Immediately mix the water and the agar by rapid but gentle to-and-fro and circular movements for 5-10 seconds, keeping the Petri dish flat on the bench throughout,
— Allow the agar to set, invert the dishes and place in the incubators.

##### 7.12.3.2.2 Incubation and Examination of the Cultures
— Incubate the two plates made with the highest dilution at 20-22°C for 3 days. These extra plates allow for the higher counts expected at this temperature,
— Incubate two of each of the remaining sets of plates at 37°C for 24 ±3 hours* and two at 20-22°C for 3 days,

---

*The incubation time at 37°C may be extended to 48 hours for some samples to satisfy the Current Monitoring programme of the Directive of the European Community (1980 b) on the Quality of Water Intended for Human Consumption (see Section 5.3).

— Count the colonies as soon as the plates are removed from the incubator. If this is not possible, keep the plates at 4°C for not longer than 24 hours.

### 7.12.3.2.3 Counting the Colonies

The best method of counting the colonies is with the aid of a colony counting apparatus with which the plates can be examined by combined reflected and obliquely transmitted artificial light against a dark background. Mechanical or electronic counting devices are useful especially if many counts have to be made. Some method of marking each colony counted on the base of the Petri dish is also advantageous.

To ensure uniformity of results the following rules should be observed:
— Count the number of colonies in the plates containing the undiluted sample, unless they exceed 300,
— Take the average of the count in each pair of plates and multiply the result by the dilution factor. If the number of colonies exceeds 300, choose a dilution level in which the number of colonies lies between 30 and 300 and count the colonies in these plates,
— If the plates made with the highest dilution contain more than 300 colonies, either try to count them and report the result as approximate, or express the count as "more than 300n colony forming units per ml", where n represents the dilution factor. If there is a gross discrepancy between the numbers of colonies in the plates, a rider should be added in the report to this effect.

## 7.13 The Test for *Pseudomonas aeruginosa*

### 7.13.1 Introduction

*Pseudomonas aeruginosa* should not be used as an indicator of faecal pollution. However, in the manufacture of food, drink and pharmaceutical products and in hospitals, it is desirable that the water should be free from *Ps. aeruginosa*. In these circumstances, and for the examination of bottled waters, the following methods of detection and enumeration may be used.

### 7.13.2 Definition

In the context of the methods, *Ps. aeruginosa* is an aerobic, Gram-negative non-sporing rod which forms oxidase and catalase, grows at 42°C but not at 4°C and shows oxidative metabolism in the test of Hugh and Leifson (1953). It reduces nitrates and nitrites, produces ammonia from the breakdown of acetamide, liquifies gelatin and hydrolyses casein but not starch. One of the most important characters is the production of the blue-green pigment pyocyanin, or the fluorescent pigment fluorescein, or both.

### 7.13.3 The Count of *Pseudomonas aeruginosa* by the Multiple Tube Method

#### 7.13.3.1 INTRODUCTION

For most waters in which it is necessary to enumerate *Ps. aeruginosa*, membrane-filtration is likely to be more suitable than the multiple tube method. The latter should be used only when membrane filtration is difficult or impossible because of the presence of excess particulate matter which blocks the pores of the membrane. Since such waters are likely to be polluted, the use of test volumes greater than 10 ml should rarely be necessary.

### 7.13.3.2 PRINCIPLE
Culture of test volumes of the sample in a liquid medium containing asparagine and ethanol, and examination for growth and pigment formation at 38-39° C. This temperature is used to inhibit the growth of other pseudomonads which are common in water and soil and which grow better at a lower temperature. Subculture to a confirmatory medium to show growth at 42° C with pigment formation, casein hydrolysis and cetrimide resistance.

### 7.13.3.3 CHOICE OF MEDIUM
Asparagine Broth with Ethanol (Drake, 1966) is recommended for isolation; each test volume of the sample is usually added to four times its volume of medium. Alternatively, for test volumes of 1 ml, Repli dishes* instead of tubes may be used with a more concentrated form of the medium. These are Petri dishes divided into 25 square compartments each of 5 ml capacity which can thus readily hold 1 ml of sample and 1 ml of medium. For confirmation, Milk Agar with Cetrimide (Brown and Foster, 1970) is recommended.

### 7.13.3.4 PROCEDURE
#### 7.13.3.4.1 Inoculation of the Medium
— After preparing the sample and making any necessary dilutions as described in 7.5, add the 10 ml test volumes to 40 ml of medium in screw-capped bottles, and the 1 ml volumes to 4 ml of medium in tubes or to 1 ml of concentrated medium in Repli-dishes.*

#### 7.13.3.4.2 Incubation and Examination of the Cultures
— Incubate at 38-39° C and examine after 48 hours for growth and fluorescence. This is best carried out in a darkened room under ultra-violet light of wavelength 350 ±20nm: it is important to exclude visible light from the UV source by means of a dark filter. Examine after 96 hours for green, blue or red pigments in the medium.
— Regard growth and pigment production as presumptive evidence for the presence of *Ps. aeruginosa*.

#### 7.13.3.4.3 Confirmation of *Ps. aeruginosa*
— Subculture from each tube, bottle or Repli dish showing fluorescence or pigmentation to a plate of Milk Agar with Cetrimide.
— Incubate at 42° C for 24 hours. Examine for growth, pigment formation and for casein hydrolysis which is shown by clearing of the medium around the colonies. *Ps. aeruginosa* grows at 42° C, hydrolyses casein and produces pyocyanin and/or fluorescein. Occasionally, non-pigmented variants of *Ps. aeruginosa* may occur.
— From the number of tubes giving a positive reaction, calculate the MPN of *Ps. aeruginosa* per 100 ml of the sample by reference to the Tables in Appendix C.

*Repli-dishes are obtainable from Sterilin, Broad Street, Teddington, Middlesex, TW11 8QZ.

— If only a qualitative result is required, report *Ps. aeruginosa* present or absent from the volume of water examined.

### 7.13.4 The Count of *Pseudomonas aeruginosa* by the Membrane Filtration Method

#### 7.13.4.1 PRINCIPLE
Filtration of a test volume of the sample through a membrane, incubation on an absorbent pad saturated with broth containing ethanol and cetrimide, and a count of the pigment-producing colonies. Subculture to a confirmatory medium to show growth at 42°C with casein hydrolysis and the production of pyocyanin or fluorescein or both.

#### 7.13.4.2 CHOICE OF MEDIUM
Modified King's A Broth (Medium 19 of Drake, 1966) is recommended for isolation, and Milk Agar with Cetrimide (Brown and Foster, 1970) as the confirmatory medium.

#### 7.13.4.3 PROCEDURE
##### 7.13.4.3.1 Incubation and Examination of the Cultures
— After preparing the sample and making any necessary dilutions as described in 7.5, filter the test volumes as in 7.8.3 and place each membrane on a pad saturated with Modified King's A Broth in a Petri dish.
— Incubate at 37°C for 48 hours in a closed container.
— Count all colonies which produce a green, blue or reddish-brown pigment and those which fluoresce under ultra-violet light. To detect fluorescence, it is advisable to use an UV light source with a dark filter to eliminate visible light. Exposure of the colonies to air for a short time enhances the pigmentation and thus makes counting easier.

##### 7.13.4.3.2 Confirmation of *Pseudomonas aeruginosa*
— Regard those colonies which clearly produce pyocyanin on the membrane as *Ps. aeruginosa*.
— To confirm other colonies, subculture them or a representative number of them to Milk Agar with Cetrimide and incubate at 42°C as described in 7.13.3.4.3.

## 8. EXAMINATION FOR PATHOGENIC ORGANISMS

## 8.1 Introduction

For technical and epidemiological reasons, the direct search for pathogenic bacteria has no place in the routine bacteriological examination of water supplies. There are occasions, however, when an investigation for faecal pathogens may be necessary as for example, when a water is suspected of transmitting disease. Also, the periodic examination of some waters for salmonellae is required by Directives of the European Community. However, the technical difficulties are still considerable in that any pathogens in the water are likely to be greatly outnumbered by the normal faecal flora or by putrifactive organisms derived from sewage. The detection of particular pathogens themselves therefore necessitates the examination by trained staff of large volumes of water by means of concentration techniques and selective enrichment media.

## 8.2 Concentration Methods

The most effective way of examining large volumes of water for pathogenic bacteria is by membrane filtration. However, because of the retention properties of membranes, this method is applicable only to very clear waters. When filtration through membranes is impracticable, especially because of turbidity, a filter-aid of powdered Kieselguhr (diatomaceous earth), such as Hyflo-supercel should be used. This is fine enough to retain most of the bacteria but is sufficiently coarse to prevent blockage so that large volumes of water can be filtered. In addition to concentrating bacteria, the method also separates them from any toxic agents which may be in solution in the sample.

### 8.2.1 Membrane Filtration
*For qualitative examination*
— Carry out the filtration as in 7.8.3. For volumes larger than 100 ml, the use of 500 ml funnels is recommended.
*For quantitative examination*
— Filter separate volumes of the sample through separate membranes: one 500 ml volume and five 100 ml volumes will give an MPN count of up to 18 organisms per litre.
— After filtration, place each membrane in a suitable enrichment medium for incubation.

### 8.2.2 Use of Filter-aid
The usual membrane filtration apparatus is used with a sterile absorbent pad in place of the membrane to act as a supporting base for the filter-aid. A small amount of a sterile aqueous suspension of the filter-aid is first filtered to form an initial layer on the absorbent pad and further suspension is then mixed with the sample and filtered. By this means the filter-aid, intimately mixed with the bacteria and debris from the water, is continuously deposited on the initial layer. This will retain more than 90 per cent of the bacteria present in the sample, although for dirty waters, greater proportions of filter-aid may be required.
*For qualitative examination*
— Place a sterile absorbent pad (7.8.2.4) in the membrane filtration apparatus.
— Take a bottle of sterile filter-aid suspension (Appendix B), shake well and pour into the funnel; apply suction and filter to form an initial layer.
— To each litre of water sample, add one well-shaken bottle of filter-aid. Mix well and filter. Mix well to resuspend the filter-aid before each addition of the sample to the funnel.
— After filtration is complete, remove the funnel carefully and transfer the absorbent pad with the layer of filter-aid to pre-enrichment medium.
— With the same medium, rinse any filter-aid adhering to the funnel into the culture vessel.

*For quantitative examination.*
— Filter a measured volume of sample as above. Add the pad with the filter-aid to 100 ml of pre-enrichment medium in a sterile flask or wide-mouthed container. Wash off any adhering filter-aid into the container with the medium from the flask.
— Mix well, and for the MPN estimation, pipette five separate volumes of 10 ml into sterile tubes, keeping the remaining 50 ml volume as a separate culture. If high counts are expected, pipette from the 50 ml volume 5 x 1 ml and 5 x 0.1 ml into separate tubes, each containing 10 ml of the pre-enrichment medium.
— Incubate at the temperature and for the time applicable to the organism sought.
— Subculture from the pre-enrichment cultures to selective enrichment media and incubate at the temperature and for the time applicable to the organism sought.
— Subculture to selective solid media to permit recognition of the particular pathogen.
— After confirmation, calculate the MPN of the pathogen in the original volume examined from the number of cultures giving a positive result.

### 8.2.3   The Sewer – Swab Technique

A useful method for the detection of pathogenic bacteria in sewage-polluted rivers, streams and other waters is the swab technique described by Moore (1948, 1950; Moore, Perry and Chard, 1952). Gauze swabs (SCA, 1983) suitably anchored by wire or other means, are immersed in the flow of water for several days. Organisms are entrapped and thus concentrated in the swab, which can then be treated in the same manner as the Hyflo-supercel concentrate. In addition, with heavily polluted waters, the liquid from the swab, and dilutions prepared from it, can be plated out directly onto agar media selective for the pathogen sought, as well as into enrichment medium.

## 8.3   The isolation and enumeration of Salmonellae (excluding *S. typhi* )

### 8.3.1   Introduction

As salmonellae are pathogenic to man their isolation and identification must be carried out only by trained personnel in properly equipped laboratories under accepted codes of safe practice (DHSS *et al.,* 1978; NWC, 1982). Although many different enrichment and selective media are described for the isolation of salmonellae (Harvey and Price, 1974, 1979), one well-tried method used for water examination in the United Kingdom is given (SCA, 1983) to enable the requirements of the Directives of the European Community to be met. This method is not suitable for the isolation of *S. typhi* because of the elevated temperature of incubation. If other media, or if lower temperatures are used, it is possible that *S. typhi* might be isolated and should this be suspected, the cultures must either be transferred immediately to a Category B1 laboratory or destroyed. Deliberate culture for *S. typhi,* or other similar pathogens, must be carried out only in a Category B1 laboratory.

## 8.3.2 Definitions

Salmonellae are Gram-negative, motile rods which are catalase-positive, oxidase-negative and facultatively anaerobic. In general, they ferment glucose, mannitol and dulcitol with the production of acid and gas but not lactose, sucrose or salicin. Citrate can usually be utilized as the sole source of carbon, urease is not produced, and the lysine-decarboxylase and $H_2S$ reactions are usually positive. *S. typhi* and *S. gallinarum* do not produce gas and anaerogenic strains of other serotypes occur occasionally.

In the context of the method, organisms which, after pre-enrichment at 37°C followed by enrichment in Muller-Kauffmann Tetrathionate Broth at 42°C, give characteristic colonies on Xylose Lysine Desoxycholate (XLD) selective agar; and colonies which give positive reactions in biochemical confirmatory media such as Lysine Iron Agar or Triple Sugar Iron Agar, are regarded as presumptive salmonellae. If these colonies are agglutinated by polyvalent 'O' and polyvalent 'H' antisera, they should be regarded as salmonellae and subjected to further serological and biochemical identification.

## 8.3.3 Principle

Concentration of organisms on a membrane filter or by means of a filter-aid followed by culture in Buffered Peptone Water to resuscitate stressed organisms; subculture to Muller-Kauffmann Tetrathionate Broth for incubation at 42°C, followed by plating on selective XLD agar; and biochemical and serological confirmation of characteristic colonies.

## 8.3.4 Choice of Medium

Media selective for salmonellae usually incorporate inhibitory substances such as selenium salts, sodium tetrathionate, brilliant green or malachite green. Selectivity can be increased further by incubation at 42°C. However, because on primary inoculation these selective media may be too inhibitory for organisms stressed in the aquatic environment, pre-enrichment in a non-selective medium such as Buffered Peptone Water, is necessary. After incubation, the enrichment cultures are plated out on selective differential media on which salmonellae form colonies with a characteristic colour and morphology. Representative colonies are then subcultured for further biochemical and serological tests.

The following media are used in this method:
— Buffered Peptone Water (Edel and Kampelmacher, 1973) for pre-enrichment,
— Muller-Kauffmann Tetrathionate Broth (Edel and Kampelmacher, 1969) for selective enrichment,
— Xylose Lysine Desoxycholate (XLD) Agar (Taylor, 1965) for selective isolation,
— Lysine Iron Agar slopes (Edwards and Fife, 1961) or Triple Sugar Iron Agar slopes and Urea Broth, for preliminary biochemical identification.

### 8.3.5 Procedure

#### 8.3.5.1 PRE-ENRICHMENT
**Membrane Filtration**
— After filtration of the sample as described in 8.2.1, place each membrane in approximately 100 ml of Buffered Peptone Water in a wide-mouthed screw-capped jar, flask or large test tube (32 x 200 mm).

**Filtration with Filter-aid**
*For qualitative examination.*
— After filtration of the sample as in 8.2.2, transfer the absorbent pad with filter-aid to approximately 100 ml of Buffered Peptone Water in a wide-mouthed container. If any filter-aid sticks to the funnel, rinse it into the container with the medium using a Pasteur pipette.

*For quantitative examination.*
— Filter a measured volume of sample as in 8.2.2. Place the filter pad with filter-aid in 100 ml of Buffered Peptone Water. Use a Pasteur pipette to rinse all the filter-aid into the medium.
— Mix well and transfer 5 separate volumes of 10 ml to sterile tubes, keeping the remaining 50 ml volume as a separate culture. If high counts are expected, pipette 5 x 1 ml and 5 x 0.1 ml volumes from the 50ml volume to separate tubes each containing 10 ml of Buffered Peptone Water,
— Incubate the containers of Buffered Peptone Water with membranes or filter aid for a resuscitation period of 24 ±2 hours at 37°C.

#### 8.3.5.2 ENRICHMENT MEDIUM : SUBCULTURE AND INCUBATION
*For qualitative examination,*
— Transfer 10 ml from the 100 ml Buffered Peptone Water pre-enrichment culture to approximately 100 ml of Muller-Kauffmann Tetrathionate Broth.
*For the quantitative filter-aid method,*
— Add each of the 10 ml Buffered Peptone Water pre-enrichment cultures to approximately 100 ml of Muller-Kauffmann Tetrathionate Broth. Alternatively if the 10 ml volumes of pre-enrichment cultures are in large test tubes or containers, the 100 ml volumes of Muller-Kauffmann medium can be added directly. Similarly, transfer 10 ml of the 50 ml volume of Buffered Peptone Water pre-enrichment culture to approximately 100 ml of Muller-Kauffmann Tetrathionate Broth.
— Incubate at 42°C ±1°C.
— After incubation for 20 ±4 hours, and also after 44 ±4 hours, subculture the growth from each tube to plates of selective XLD agar.

For enrichment culture, other selective media such as Selenite F (Leifson 1936; Hobbs and Allison 1945a, b) or Rappaport's Broth (Rappaport, Konforti and Navon 1956; Vassiliadis, Trichopoulos, Papadakis and Politi 1970; Harvey, Price and Xirouchaki 1979) may be used. If a medium containing selenite is used, the ratio of the inoculum taken from the pre-enrichment culture to the volume of enrichment medium should be about 1:10, as with Muller-Kauffmann Tetrathionate Broth (Jameson, 1961). If, however, Rappaport's Broth is used, the inoculum ratio should be about

1:100; for example 1 ml of pre-enrichment culture to 100 ml of Rappaport medium. A large inoculum, without a corresponding increase in the volume of enrichment broth, destroys the selectivity of Rappaport's medium (Rappaport et al, 1956; Harvey and Price 1980). This medium should be incubated at 37°C, but media containing selenite and Muller-Kauffmann Tetrathionate Broth may, with advantage, be incubated at 42°C-43°C.

For selective plating, Brilliant-green MacConkey Agar (Harvey 1956), Deoxycholate Citrate Agar (Leifson 1935; Hynes 1942), Bismuth Sulphite Iron Agar (Wilson & Blair, 1927) or one of its modifications (Cook, 1952; de Loureiro, 1942; McCoy, 1962) may be used. Some microbiologists like to age their bismuth sulphite medium to render it less inhibitory; others prefer to use it freshly prepared. An advantage of this medium over others is its ability to detect subgenus III salmonellae, many of which are able to ferment lactose (Harvey, Price and Hall 1973).

### 8.3.5.3 ISOLATION AND IDENTIFICATION ON SELECTIVE XLD AGAR

— Incubate the XLD plates at 37°C for 18-24 hours.
— Examine them for characteristic colonies by reflected and transmitted light with a hand lens or, if necessary, a low-magnification microscope. On XLD agar, salmonellae form red colonies with black centres; these often look more like black colonies with a red periphery.

### 8.3.5.4 CONFIRMATION

— Subculture characteristic colonies from each plate using a straight wire to confirmatory media such as Lysine Iron Agar, or Triple Sugar Iron Agar together with Urea Broth. Incubate at 37°C for 18-24 hours,
— Regard cultures which give characteristic reactions in these confirmatory media as presumptive salmonellae (Tables 2 and 3). Alternatively, one or other of the multitest differential identification systems available may be used,
— Carry out, if possible, serological confirmation of presumptive salmonella cultures with polyvalent 'O' and 'H' antisera. If positive, subculture to Nutrient Agar slopes for submission to a reference centre for final confirmation and serological identification.

Table 2. Reactions in Lysine Iron Agar

| Genus | Slope | Butt | H₂S |
|---|---|---|---|
| Arizona | Alk | Alk | + |
| Salmonella | Alk | Alk | + |
| Proteus | Red | A | + or − |
| Providencia | Red | A | − |
| Citrobacter | Alk | A | + |
| Escherichia | Alk | A or NC | − |
| Shigella | Alk | A | − |
| Klebsiella | Alk | Alk | − |
| Enterobacter | Alk | A | − |

A = Acid (yellow)
Alk = Alkali (purple)
NC = No change
H₂S+ = Blackening

Table 3. Reactions in Triple Sugar Iron Agar and Urea Broth.

| Organism | Butt | Slope | H₂S | Urea Broth |
|---|---|---|---|---|
| Klebsiella sp. | A G | A | — | + or − |
| Enterobacter aerogenes | A G | A | — | — |
| Escherichia coli | A G | A | — | — |
| Proteus vulgaris | A G | A | + | + |
| Proteus morganii | A or A G | N C or Alk | — | + |
| Shigella sp | A | N C or Alk | — | — |
| Salmonella typhi | A | N C or Alk | + (weak) | — |
| Salmonella paratyphi B and other salmonellae | A G | N C or Alk | + | — |

AG      =   Acid (yellow) and gas formation
A        =   Acid (yellow)
NC      =   No change
Alk      =   Alkaline (red)
H₂S+   =   Blackening
Urea Broth +   =   Alkaline (red)
              — =   No change

## 8.4   Other pathogenic organisms

Occasionally it may be necessary to examine samples of water suspected of transmitting disease for pathogens such as shigella, campylobacter, typhoid organisms or others. It is important to collect such samples as soon as possible, and take account of any treatment, environmental, medical and epidemiological factors that may be concerned. Close liaison with the Medical Officer for Environmental Health and the Public Health Laboratory Service in England and Wales, or their equivalent elsewhere, is essential to ensure that the main efforts are directed towards the most likely causal organisms, and that subsequent comparison may be made with clinical isolates. It is neither possible nor desirable to prescribe standard procedures for the detection of all possible pathogenic micro-organisms — if only because of the many different methods and media, and variations of them, used by experienced medical and other microbiologists. However, the methods of concentration given in Section 8.2 may be used, and should be followed by cultural techniques and media appropriate for the organisms sought. As a guide, methods suitable for the detection of certain pathogens, such as S. typhi and vibrios, may be found in the Monograph Series of the Public Health Laboratory Service. If waterborne disease is suspected, then, in addition to intensive bacteriological examination of the supply concerned, large volumes (several litres) of the water, both before treatment and as distributed, should be taken as soon as possible from a number of agreed sampling points, and repeated on several subsequent occasions. These samples should each be divided into two or more parts and one kept at 4°C and the other at room temperature in the dark for subsequent further investigations, including where necessary, examination for viruses and parasites at special laboratories.

# Appendices

## Appendix A : Laboratory Glassware

### Specifications

**SAMPLE BOTTLES**
Sample bottles should be of good quality glass or plastic, free from toxic substances. They should be provided by the laboratory performing the examination and should be used exclusively for bacteriological purposes. The size of the bottle depends on the number of tests to be carried out and the methods used. A capacity of about 300 ml is sufficient for most routine purposes. The bottles should be fitted with ground-glass stoppers or screw-caps fitted when necessary with silicone rubber liners which will withstand repeated sterilization at 160°C.

**PIPETTES**
Pipettes should conform to British Standard Specification BS 700:1976. The 1 ml and 10 ml sizes should be of the straight-sided, total delivery (blowout) type. Alternatively, automatic pipettes with sterile disposable tips may be used.

**GLASSWARE FOR LIQUID MEDIA**
The 50 ml volumes of double-strength medium required for the MPN method should be distributed in screw-capped bottles of at least 125 ml capacity, and the 10 ml volumes in test-tubes 150mm x 19mm, with a capacity of about 30 ml. For the 5 ml volumes of single-strength medium and for most other liquid media, tubes 150mm x 16mm with a capacity of about 22 ml are suitable. When inner (Durham) fermentation tubes are needed to show gas formation, a suitable size for the 5 and 10 ml volumes of medium is 35mm x 8mm, and for the 50 ml volumes, 75mm x 10mm. When media need to be stored for several weeks, screw-capped containers should be used.

**PETRI DISHES**
It is important that Petri dishes used for colony counts should be of a standard size to ensure that the surface area and depth of the medium are always constant. Glass dishes should conform to British Standard Specification BS 611:1978. Sterile disposable (for example, polystyrene) Petri dishes are also suitable for general use.

### Cleaning and Preparation
After use pipettes should be placed in a jar of disinfectant such as hypochlorite solution containing 1000 mg/l of free chlorine, and left for one hour before rinsing several times. They should then be given a final rinse in distilled water, dried and packed in metal canisters for sterilization. Plugging pipettes with non-absorbent cotton wool will help to reduce cross-

contamination. It is advisable to clean glass pipettes periodically with a non-toxic detergent or acid and then rinse thoroughly.

Test-tubes, bottles and flasks should be autoclaved after use and then cleaned with a brush, washed in water with a non-toxic detergent, rinsed in clean water and finally in distilled water.

Test-tubes and flasks should be plugged with non-absorbent cotton wool or covered with closely-fitting aluminium or polypropylene caps. The necks and stoppers of bottles should be covered with paper or foil to prevent contamination.

Glass Petri dishes, after autoclaving, should be boiled in water with a little washing soda or detergent to remove all traces of agar, then rinsed in running water and finally in distilled water.

## Sterilization of Glassware

Glassware may be sterilized in a hot-air oven at 160° C for 1 hour. If this temperature is exceeded, the exposure time may be reduced proportionately. A temperature above 170° C should be avoided since it tends to char organic matter and render cotton wool friable. Alternatively, bottles and tubes may be autoclaved at 121° C for 20 minutes. If bottles with ground-glass stoppers are used, a strip of paper or foil about 75 x 10mm should be inserted between the stopper and the neck of the bottle before sterilization. This prevents jamming of the stopper and cracking of the glass on cooling.

# Appendix B : Media and Reagents

## Choice of Constituents

### PEPTONE
In the preparation of media, unless a particular grade is specified, any bacteriological peptone may be used which forms a clear solution and does not precipitate when alkali is added to adjust the pH.

### AGAR
In the instructions which follow, a satisfactory gel strength with the concentration of agar in the medium is assumed. This may be varied according to the quality of the agar available. It is also assumed that the agar forms a solution which remains clear enough for filtration to be unnecessary.

### BILE SALTS
The term bile salts includes sodium taurocholate and sodium tauroglycocholate. Different preparations of bile salts vary in their inhibitory properties; each new batch should be tested against a known satisfactory product and the concentration adjusted accordingly.

### DISTILLED WATER
Where distilled water is specified, a glass still should be used; deionized water may be used instead.

### DEHYDRATED MEDIA
Some of the media described are available commercially in dehydrated form and should be reconstituted according to the manufacturers' instructions.

### STERILIZATION OF MEDIA
A time-temperature combination of 121° C for 15 minutes is usually specified for many bacteriological purposes. However, a temperature of 115° C for a minimum of 10 minutes is recommended for most media used in water examination. With volumes of one litre or more, the time but not the temperature should be increased.

### STORAGE OF MEDIA
In general, after sterilization most media in sealed containers may be stored safely for several months at room temperature provided they are kept in the dark. Media dispensed aseptically may be kept at 4-10° C for up to one month; before use, they should be inspected carefully for any untoward signs such as contamination or excessive evaporation. Most reagents are best kept at 4° C.

## Preparation of Media and Reagents

### BASIC MEDIA
#### Nutrient Broth

| | |
|---|---|
| Meat extract | 10g |
| Peptone | 10g |
| Sodium chloride | 5g |
| Distilled water | 1000ml |

Add the ingredients to the water and heat to dissolve. Adjust the pH to about 8.2 with a solution of sodium hydroxide and boil for 10 minutes. Clarify by filtration and adjust to pH 7.2-7.4. Dispense in bottles or tubes and autoclave at 115°C for 10 minutes.

#### Nutrient Agar
Nutrient Broth gelled by the addition of agar.

#### Blood Agar
Nutrient Agar with the addition of 5 per cent (v/v) horse blood.

### MEDIA FOR COLIFORM ORGANISMS
#### Improved Formate Lactose Glutamate Medium*
(PHLS 1969, modified from Gray, 1964).

| Double-strength medium: | |
|---|---|
| Lactose | 20g |
| L(+) Glutamic acid sodium salt | 12.7g |
| L(+) Arginine monohydrochloride | 0.048g |
| L(−) Aspartic acid | 0.04g |
| L(−) Cystine | 0.04g |
| Sodium formate | 0.5g |
| Dipotassium hydrogen phosphate | 1.8g |
| Ammonium chloride | 5g |
| Magnesium sulphate ($MgSO_4$. $7H_2O$) | 0.2g |
| Calcium chloride ($CaCl_2$. $2H_2O$) | 0.02g |
| Ferric citrate scales | 0.02g |
| Thiamin (Aneurin hydrochloride) | 0.002g |
| Nicotinic acid | 0.002g |
| Pantothenic acid | 0.002g |
| Bromocresol purple (1 per cent w/v ethanolic solution) | 2ml |
| Distilled water to | 1000ml |

The medium is most conveniently prepared in quantities of 10 litres or more. If it is not to be distributed in tubes immediately, the lactose and thiamine should be omitted and added immediately before dispensing. Several of the ingredients are more conveniently added as separate solutions and these should be prepared as follows:

---

*This is available in dehydrated form as Minerals Modified Glutamate Medium from Oxoid, Wade Road, Basingstoke, Hants RG2 40PW. It may also require pH adjustment.

## SOLUTION 1

| | |
|---|---|
| L(+) Arginine monohydrochloride | 0.4g |
| L(−) Aspartic acid | 0.48g |
| Distilled water | 50ml |
| Heat to dissolve | |

## SOLUTION 2

| | |
|---|---|
| L(−) Cystine | 0.4g |
| 5N Sodium hydroxide | 10ml |
| Distilled water | 90ml |
| Heat to dissolve | |

## SOLUTION 3

| | |
|---|---|
| Nicotinic acid | 0.02g |
| Pantothenic acid | 0.02g |
| Distilled water | 5ml |
| Dissolve in the cold | |

## SOLUTION 4

| | |
|---|---|
| Ferric citrate scales | 0.2g |
| Distilled water | 10ml |
| Heat to dissolve | |

## SOLUTION 5

| | |
|---|---|
| Calcium chloride ($CaCl_2$. $2H_2O$) | 5g |
| Distilled Water | 100ml |
| Concentrated hydrochloric acid | 0.1ml |

Dissolve in the cold and sterilize at 121°C for 20 minutes. Keep as a stock solution.

## SOLUTION 6

Sterile 0.1 per cent solution of thiamin in distilled water. This is best prepared by adding the contents of an ampoule (100mg) aseptically to 99ml of sterile distilled water. The solution should be kept at 4°C and any remaining discarded after 6 weeks.

To prepare 10 litres of double-strength medium, dissolve the appropriate quantities of L(+) glutamic acid sodium salt, sodium formate, dipotassium hydrogen phosphate, ammonium chloride and magnesium sulphate in 9 litres of hot distilled water. Then add the whole of Solutions 1,2,3 and 4 and 4 ml of Solution 5. Adjust the pH to 6.8 or higher if necessary, so that the final pH after completion and sterilization is 6.7. If the same equipment and methods of sterilization are used, the same change in pH should always occur on sterilization. Some preliminary trials may be necessary to establish the correct pH prior to sterilization.

After adjustment of pH, add 20ml of 1 per cent ethanolic solution of bromocresol purple. Make up the final volume to 10 litres. This should require about another 810ml of distilled water. If the bulk of the medium is not required for immediate use, bottle in 500ml volumes and autoclave at 115°C for 10 minutes. For use, add the necessary amount of lactose and thiamin (Solution 6), allow to dissolve and then distribute in 10ml and 50ml volumes. Each tube or bottle should contain a Durham fermentation tube. Sterilize at 115°C for 10 minutes or in a steamer at 100°C for 30 minutes on three successive days.

Single-strength medium:

Prepare single-strength medium by diluting the double-strength medium with an equal volume of distilled water and distribute in 5ml volumes in tubes containing an inverted fermentation (Durham) tube. Sterilize at 115°C for 10 minutes or steam at 100°C for 30 minutes on three successive days.

### Lauryl Tryptose (Lactose) Broth (APHA, 1976)

Double-strength medium:

| | |
|---|---|
| Tryptose | 40g |
| Lactose | 10g |
| Sodium chloride | 10g |
| Di-potassium hydrogen phosphate | 5.5g |
| Potassium dihydrogen phosphate | 5.5g |
| Sodium lauryl sulphate — specially pure (BDH 44244) | 0.2g |
| Distilled water | 1000ml |

Add the tryptose, sodium choloride, lactose and phosphates to the water and warm to dissolve. Add the sodium lauryl sulphate and mix gently to avoid froth. Adjust to pH 6.8. Prepare single-strength medium by dilution of the double-strength medium with an equal volume of distilled water.

Distribute single-strength medium in 5ml volumes and double-strength medium in 10ml and 50ml volumes. Each tube or bottle should contain an inverted fermentation (Durham) tube. Autoclave at 115°C for 10 minutes.

### Lauryl Tryptose Mannitol Broth with Tryptophan (PHLS/SCA, 1980c)

| | |
|---|---|
| Tryptose | 20g |
| Mannitol | 5g |
| Sodium chloride | 5g |
| Di-potassium hydrogen phosphate | 2.75g |
| Potassium dihydrogen phosphate | 2.75g |
| Sodium lauryl sulphate | 0.1g |
| L(−) Tryptophan | 0.2g |
| Distilled water | 1000ml |

Add the tryptose, sodium chloride, mannitol, phosphates and tryptophan to the water and warm to dissolve. Add the sodium lauryl sulphate and mix gently to avoid froth. Adjust to pH 6.8. Distribute in 5ml volumes in tubes containing an inverted fermentation (Durham) tube. Autoclave at 115°C for 10 minutes.

### Brilliant-green Lactose Bile Broth

| | |
|---|---|
| Peptone | 10g |
| Lactose | 10g |
| Ox Bile (dehydrated) | 20g |

Brilliant-green (0.1 per cent w/v aqueous solution)   13ml
Distilled water to                                    1000ml
Dissolve the peptone in 500ml distilled water. Add the 20g of dehydrated ox bile dissolved in 200ml of distilled water: this solution should have a pH between 7.0 and 7.5. Make up with distilled water to approximately 975ml. Add the lactose and adjust the pH to 7.4. Add the brilliant-green solution and make up the volume with distilled water to 1000ml.

Distribute 5ml volumes in test tubes containing inverted fermentation (Durham) tubes and autoclave at 115°C for 10 minutes.

## Tryptone Water for Indole Reaction

Certain peptones which give satisfactory results in tests at 37°C are not satisfactory for the indole test at 44°C (Burman 1955). Oxoid tryptone has been found satisfactory and is recommended.

Tryptone (Oxoid)                                      20g
Sodium chloride                                       5g
Distilled water                                       1000ml

Dissolve the ingredients in the water and adjust the reaction to pH 7.5. Distribute in 5ml volumes and autoclave at 115°C for 10 minutes.

## Membrane Enriched Teepol Broth (DHSS *et al.* 1969)

Peptone                                               40g
Yeast extract                                         6g
Lactose                                               30g
Phenol red (0.4 per cent w/v aqueous solution)        50ml
Teepol 610                                            4ml
Distilled water                                       1000ml

Add the peptone and yeast extract to the water and steam to dissolve; add the lactose, phenol red and Teepol afterwards and mix gently to avoid froth. The final pH of the medium should be 7.4 to 7.5 and it may be necessary to adjust the pH to about 7.6 before sterilization in order to achieve this. Distribute in screw-capped bottles and autoclave at 115°C for 10 minutes.

## Membrane Lauryl Sulphate Broth (PHLS/SCA, 1980b)

Peptone                                               40g
Yeast Extract                                         6g
Lactose                                               30g
Phenol red (0.4 per cent w/v aqueous solution)        50ml
Sodium lauryl sulphate — specially pure
   (BDH 44244)                                        1g
Distilled water                                       1000ml

Add the ingredients to the water and mix gently to avoid froth. The final pH of the medium should be 7.4 to 7.5 and it may be necessary to adjust the pH to about 7.6 before sterilization to achieve this. Distribute in screw-capped bottles and autoclave at 115°C for 10 minutes.

## MacConkey Agar

Bile salts                                            5g

| | |
|---|---|
| Peptone | 20g |
| Lactose | 10g |
| Sodium chloride | 5g |
| Agar | 12g |
| Neutral red (1 per cent w/v aqueous solution) | 5ml |
| Distilled water | 1000ml |

Add the ingredients to the water and steam to dissolve. Distribute into screw-capped bottles and autoclave at 115°C for 10 minutes. For use, melt in steam and pour into sterile Petri dishes, using 15ml of medium for each dish.

## MacConkey Broth

Double-strength medium:

| | |
|---|---|
| Bile salts | 10g |
| Peptone | 40g |
| Lactose | 20g |
| Sodium chloride | 10g |
| Bromocresol purple (1 per cent w/v ethanolic solution) | 2ml |
| Distilled water | 1000ml |

Dissolve the peptone, sodium chloride and bile salts in the water by heating and store at 4°C overnight. Filter while still cold, add the lactose and dissolve. Adjust to pH 7.4 and add the bromocresol purple.
Single-strength medium.

Prepare single-strength medium by dilution of the double-strength medium with an equal volume of distilled water or make afresh using half the concentration of ingredients.

Distribute single-strength medium in 5ml volumes and double-strength medium in 10ml and 50ml volumes in tubes or bottles each containing an inverted fermentation (Durham) tube. Autoclave at 115°C for 10 minutes.

## Lactose Peptone Water

| | |
|---|---|
| Peptone | 10g |
| Sodium chloride | 5g |
| Lactose | 10g |
| Phenol red (0.4 per cent w/v aqueous solution) | 2.5ml |
| (or Andrade's indicator) | (10ml) |
| Distilled water | 1000ml |

Dissolve the ingredients in the water and adjust to pH 7.5. Add the phenol-red indicator and distribute in 5ml volumes into tubes containing inverted fermentation (Durham) tubes. Alternatively, adjust to pH 6.8 — 7.0, and add the Andrade's indicator. Autoclave at 110°C for 10 minutes. Alternatively, steam for 20 minutes on each of three successive days. Test for sterility by incubation at 37°C for 24 hours.

## Andrade's Indicator

This is prepared by dissolving 0.5g of acid fuchsin in 100ml of distilled water. Add 17ml of Normal sodium hydroxide solution and leave at room temperature overnight. The solution should be straw coloured the following morning. If it is at all brownish, add a little more sodium hydroxide solution and allow to stand again. This solution is strongly alkaline, and consequently media to which it is added should be adjusted previously to a pH of about 6.8.

### Glucose Phosphate Medium (For Methyl-red and Voges Proskauer tests)

| | |
|---|---|
| Peptone | 5g |
| Glucose | 5g |
| Dipotassium hydrogen phosphate | 5g |
| Distilled water | 1000ml |

Dissolve the ingredients in the water and adjust to pH 7.5. Distribute in 4ml volumes in test tubes or screw-capped bottles and autoclave at 110°C for 10 minutes or steam on three successive days. Test for sterility by incubation at 37°C for 24 hours.

### Citrate Medium (Koser, 1923)

| | |
|---|---|
| Sodium chloride | 5g |
| Magnesium sulphate (Mg $SO_4.7H_2O$) | 0.2g |
| Ammonium dihydrogen phosphate | 1g |
| Dipotassium hydrogen phosphate | 1g |
| Citric acid | 2g |
| Distilled water | 1000ml |

Dissolve the ingredients in the water and adjust to pH 6.8 with Normal sodium hydroxide solution. Some workers add 20ml of 0.4 per cent w/v aqueous solution of bromothymol blue to each litre of medium. Distribute in 5ml volumes in screw-capped containers and autoclave at 115°C for 10 minutes.

### Citrate Agar Medium (Simmons, 1926).

Solidify Koser's Citrate Medium with bromothymol blue indicator by the addition of 1.2 per cent agar.

## MEDIA FOR FAECAL STREPTOCOCCI*

### Glucose Azide Broth* (Hannay and Norton, 1947)

Double-strength medium:

| | |
|---|---|
| Peptone | 20g |
| Sodium chloride | 10g |
| Dipotassium hydrogen phosphate | 10g |
| Potassium dihydrogen phosphate | 4g |
| Glucose | 10g |
| Yeast extract | 6g |
| Sodium azide* | 0.5g |
| Bromocresol purple (1.6 per cent w/v ethanolic solution) | 4ml |
| Distilled water | 1000ml |

---

*NOTE — Sodium azide is highly toxic if ingested or inhaled and care must be taken when handling it. Solutions containing azide should not be discharged through metal pipework or ·lrains as explosive compounds may be formed. Azides can be decomposed by an excess of a nitrite solution.

72

Dissolve all the ingredients in the water and adjust to pH 6.6 - 6.8. Prepare single-strength medium by dilution of the double-strength medium with an equal volume of distilled water or make afresh using half the concentration of ingredients. Distribute single-strength medium in 5ml volumes and double-strength medium in 10ml and 50ml volumes. Autoclave at 115° C for 10 minutes.

### Membrane Enterococcus Agar* (Slanetz and Bartley, 1957)

| | |
|---|---|
| Tryptose | 20g |
| Yeast extract | 5g |
| Glucose | 2g |
| Dipotassium hydrogen phosphate | 4g |
| Sodium azide* | 0.4g |
| Agar | 12g |
| 2,3,5 - triphenyltetrazolium chloride (TTC) | 10ml |
| (1 per cent w/v aqueous solution) | |
| Distilled water | 1000ml |

Steam the ingredients to dissolve. The pH should be 7.2 without the need for adjustment. Add the TTC indicator solution, sterilized by filtration, and pour the medium directly into Petri dishes without further sterilization. The medium with or without TTC should not be stored and re-melted, but poured plates may be kept at 4° C for up to 6 months if placed in a sealed container to prevent drying.

### Tyrosine Sorbitol Thallous Acetate Agar§ (Mead, 1963)

Lower basal layer:

| | |
|---|---|
| Peptone | 10g |
| Yeast extract | 1g |
| Sorbitol | 2g |
| Tyrosine | 5g |
| Agar | 12g |
| 2,3,5 - triphenyltetrazolium chloride (TTC) | |
| (1 per cent w/v aqueous solution) | 10ml |
| Thallous acetate§ | 1g |
| Distilled water | 1000ml |

Prepare the medium for the lower basal layer by dissolving the first five ingredients in the water and autoclaving at 115° C for 10 minutes. Adjust the pH to 6.2 and add the filter-sterilized solutions of TTC and the thallous acetate. Pour as a shallow layer in Petri dishes and allow to set.

Upper layer:
Prepare the medium for the upper layer in the same way as the basal

---

*NOTE — Sodium azide is highly toxic if ingested or inhaled and care must be taken when handling it. Solutions containing azide should not be discharged through metal pipework or drains as explosive compounds may be formed. Azides can be decomposed by an excess of a nitrite solution.

§NOTE — Thallous acetate is highly toxic if ingested or inhaled. It gives off toxic fumes if heated in the solid state, and is also inflammable. With hypochlorites, thallic chloride is formed which is volatile in steam and toxic. Care must therefore be taken when handling this substance.

layer but add an extra 4g of tyrosine whilst the medium is still hot. This extra tyrosine remains in suspension whereas the original tyrosine dissolves completely during autoclaving. When sufficiently cool, pour the medium for the upper layer to obtain a uniform suspension before it sets.

## Bile Agar 40 per cent (Cowan, 1974)

| | |
|---|---|
| Ox bile (dehydrated) | 40g† |
| Serum (sterile) | 50ml |
| Nutrient agar | 1000ml |

Melt the nutrient agar, add the ox bile and mix to dissolve. Autoclave at 115°C for 10 minutes. Cool to about 55°C and add the serum aseptically. Mix gently and distribute in bottles, tubes or plates.

† Note this is equivalent to 400ml fresh bile.

## Bile Aesculin Azide Agar*

| | |
|---|---|
| Ox bile (dehydrated) | 10g |
| Peptone | 10g |
| Meat extract | 10g |
| Sodium chloride | 5g |
| Sodium azide* | 0.15g |
| Ferric ammonium citrate | 0.5g |
| Aesculin | 1g |
| Agar | 10g |
| Distilled water | 1000ml |

Steam to dissolve the ingredients and adjust to pH 7.0. Sterilize at 115°C for 10 minutes. Pour into Petri dishes and store at 4°C in sealed containers to prevent drying.

## Glucose Phenolphthalein Broth (Clarke, 1953)

Glucose Broth:

| | |
|---|---|
| Meat extract | 10g |
| Peptone | 10g |
| Sodium chloride | 5g |
| Distilled water | 1000ml |

Dissolve the ingredients in the water and adjust the pH to 7.2 - 7.4. Sterilize at 115°C for 10 minutes.

Prepare a 20 per cent w/v aqueous solution of glucose and sterilize by filtration. Add 50ml aseptically to 950ml of the nutrient broth.

Glycine Buffer:

| | |
|---|---|
| Glycine | 0.6g |
| Sodium chloride | 0.35g |
| Distilled water, freshly boiled | 60ml |
| 0.1N Sodium hydroxide | 40ml |

---

*NOTE — Sodium azide is highly toxic if ingested or inhaled and care must be taken when handling it. Solutions containing azide should not be discharged through metal pipework or drains as explosive compounds may be formed. Azides can be decomposed by an excess of a nitrite solution.

Dissolve the glycine and sodium chloride in the hot water and then add the sodium hydroxide.

Complete Medium:

| | |
|---|---|
| Glucose Broth | 900ml |
| Glycine Buffer | 100ml |
| Phenolphthalein (0.2 per cent w/v aqueous solution) | 5ml |

Mix and keep overnight in the refrigerator in a stoppered flask. Sterilize by filtration and distribute aseptically into sterile 5ml screw-capped bottles leaving as little air space as possible. Incubate at 37°C overnight to check sterility and discard any bottle showing growth or not having a definite pink colour.

### Salt Broth (Cowan, 1974)
(Nutrient Broth with 6.5 per cent w/v Sodium Chloride)

| | |
|---|---|
| Meat extract | 10g |
| Peptone | 10g |
| Sodium chloride | 65g |
| Distilled water | 1000ml |

Dissolve the ingredients in the water, adjust the pH to 7.2 - 7.4. Distribute in 5ml volumes and sterilize at 115°C for 10 minutes.

## MEDIA FOR SULPHITE-REDUCING CLOSTRIDIA
### Differential Reinforced Clostridial Medium (Gibbs and Freame, 1965)
Basal Medium — Single Strength:

| | |
|---|---|
| Peptone | 10g |
| Meat extract | 10g |
| Sodium acetate (hydrated) | 5g |
| Yeast extract | 1.5g |
| Soluble starch | 1g |
| Glucose | 1g |
| L(−) Cysteine hydrochloride | 0.5g |
| Distilled water | 1000ml |

Add the peptone, meat extract, sodium acetate and yeast extract to 800ml of the water. Dissolve the starch in the remaining 200ml, first making a cold slurry with a little of the water, boiling the rest and stirring it into the paste. Add the glucose and cysteine and dissolve. Adjust the pH to 7.1. - 7.2., distribute 25ml volumes in universal screw-capped bottles and autoclave at 121°C for 15 minutes.

Basal Medium — Double Strength:

Prepare in the same way using twice the quantity of ingredients; distribute 10ml volumes in universal screw-capped bottles and 50ml volumes in 125ml screw-capped bottles.

Sodium Sulphite and Ferric Citrate Solutions:

Prepare solutions of sodium sulphite (anhydrous) 4 per cent (w/v) and ferric citrate (scales) 7 per cent (w/v) in distilled water. Heat the latter to dissolve. Sterilize by filtration. The solutions may be stored at 4°C for up to 14 days.

**Final Medium:**

On the day of use, mix equal volumes of the two solutions. To give final concentrations of 0.4 per cent sodium sulphite and 0.07 per cent ferric citrate, add 0.5ml of the mixture to each 25ml volume of the single-strength basal medium, freshly steamed and cooled to exclude dissolved oxygen. To each 10ml and 50ml volume of double-strength medium, add 0.4ml and 2.0ml respectively of the the sulphite-iron mixture.

**Membrane Clostridial Agar** (Modified from Burman, Oliver and Stevens, 1969)

**Basal Medium:**

| | |
|---|---|
| Meat extract | 3g |
| Peptone | 10g |
| Glucose | 20g |
| Sodium chloride | 5g |
| Agar | 15g |
| Distilled water | 1000ml |

Dissolve the ingredients by steaming and adjust to pH 7.6 with Normal sodium hydroxide. Distribute in 18ml volumes in screw-capped (Universal) containers. Sterilize by autoclaving at 121°C for 15 minutes.

**Solution A: Aqueous Sodium Sulphite  (10 per cent w/v)**

| | |
|---|---|
| Sodium sulphite (anhydrous) | 10g |
| Distilled water | 100ml |

Dissolve and sterilize by autoclaving at 121°C for 15 minutes.

**Solution B: Aqueous Ferrous Sulphate  (8 per cent w/v)**

| | |
|---|---|
| Ferrous sulphate (crystalline) | 8g |
| Distilled water | 100ml |

Dissolve by steaming and sterilize by autoclaving at 121°C for 15 minutes.

**Preparation of Final Medium**

For use, melt 18ml of the basal medium. Cool to 50°C and add aseptically 1.0ml of Solution A and 0.1ml of Solution B. Mix gently and pour carefully over the membrane in a Petri dish.

**Litmus Milk**

To milk prepared from skimmed-milk powder, add sufficient 10 per cent (w/v) aqueous solution of litmus to give a bluish-purple colour. Distribute in 5ml volumes in screw-capped bottles and autoclave at 115°C for 10 minutes.

## MEDIUM FOR COLONY COUNTS

### Yeast Extract Agar

| | |
|---|---|
| Yeast extract | 3g |
| Peptone | 5g |
| Agar | 12g |
| Distilled water | 1000ml |

Dissolve the yeast extract and peptone in the water. Adjust the reaction to pH 7.3. Add the agar and steam to dissolve. Distribute in 15ml amounts in tubes or universal containers or larger volumes in screw-capped bottles. Autoclave at 115°C for 10 minutes.

# MEDIA FOR *PSEUDOMONAS AERUGINOSA*

## Modified King's A Broth (Medium 19 of Drake, 1966)

| | |
|---|---|
| Peptone | 20g |
| Ethanol | 25ml |
| Potassium sulphate, anhydrous | 10g |
| Magnesium chloride, anhydrous | 1.4g |
| (or $MgCl_2.6H_2O$) | (2.9g) |
| Cetrimide (Cetyltrimethyl ammonium bromide BDH 27665) | 0.5g |
| Distilled water to | 1000ml |

Steam to dissolve the ingredients. Distribute in screw-capped bottles and autoclave at 115°C for 10 minutes. Remove the bottles from the autoclave promptly after this sterilization cycle has been completed in order to prevent excessive loss of ethanol from the medium. Alternatively, add filter-sterilized ethanol aseptically to the sterile broth. The final pH should be approximately 7.2; no adjustment is usually necessary.

## Asparagine Broth with Ethanol (Medium 10 of Drake, 1966)

| | Single strength medium | Concentrate for use in Repli-dishes* |
|---|---|---|
| L ( − ) Asparagine | 2g | 3.2g |
| L ( − ) Proline | 1g | 1.6g |
| Dipotassium hydrogen phosphate, anhydrous | 1.0g | 1.6g |
| Magnesium sulphate (Mg $SO_4. 7H_2O$) | 0.5g | 0.8g |
| Potassium sulphate, anhydrous | 10g | 16g |
| Ethanol | 25ml | 40ml |
| Distilled water to | 1000ml | 1000ml |

Steam the ingredients to dissolve. Distribute the single strength medium in 4ml volumes in screw-capped bijoux bottles, and the 40ml volumes in bottles of 50-100ml capacity; dispense the concentrated medium in larger bottles for storage. Autoclave at 115°C for 10 minutes. Remove the bottles promptly from the autoclave after this sterilization cycle has been completed in order to prevent excessive loss of ethanol from the medium. Alternatively, add filter-sterilized ethanol aseptically to the sterile medium. The final pH should be approximately 7.2; no adjustment is usually necessary.

## Milk Agar with Cetrimide (Brown and Foster, 1970)

Yeast extract broth:

| | |
|---|---|
| Yeast extract | 0.75g |
| Peptone | 2.5g |
| Sodium chloride | 1.25g |
| Distilled water | 250ml |

Dissolve the ingredients and adjust the pH to 7.2 - 7.4. Autoclave at 115°C for 10 minutes.

---

*Repli-dishes are obtainable from Sterilin, Broad Street, Teddington, Middlesex, TW11 8QZ.

77

Final medium:

| | |
|---|---|
| Skimmed milk powder* | 100g |
| Yeast extract broth | 250ml |
| Agar | 15g |
| Cetrimide (Cetyltrimethyl-ammonium bromide — BDH 27665) | 0.3g |
| Distilled water | 750ml |

Add the Cetrimide and agar to the yeast extract broth and steam to dissolve the agar. Mix the skimmed milk powder and distilled water by stirring. Autoclave both solutions separately at 121°C for 5 minutes and remove them promptly from the autoclave after this sterilization cycle has been completed in order to prevent caramelization of the lactose in the milk. Cool to 50-55°C, mix aseptically and pour into Petri dishes. Store the plates at 4°C for not longer than 4 weeks in sealed containers to prevent drying.

*Thermophile-free skimmed milk powder for bacteriological purposes is available commercially.

## TRANSPORT MEDIUM

**Membrane Transport Medium** (Panezai, Macklin and Coles, 1965)

| | |
|---|---|
| Peptone | 0.2g |
| Sodium chloride | 0.1g |
| Sodium benzoate | 4g |
| Distilled water | 1000ml |

Dissolve the ingredients and adjust the pH to 7.5. Distribute in tubes or bottles in convenient volumes and autoclave at 115°C for 10 minutes.

## MEDIA FOR SALMONELLAE

**Buffered Peptone Water** (Edel and Kampelmacher, 1973)

| | |
|---|---|
| Peptone | 10g |
| Sodium chloride | 5g |
| Disodium hydrogen phosphate, anhydrous | 3.5g |
| Potassium dihydrogen phosphate, anhydrous | 1.5g |
| Distilled water | 1000ml |

Dissolve the ingredients. Distribute in bulk quantities in screw-capped bottles and autoclave at 115°C for 10 minutes. The final pH should be approximately 7.2. No adjustment is usually necessary.

**Muller-Kauffmann Tetrathionate Broth** (Edel and Kampelmacher, 1969)

Broth base:

| | |
|---|---|
| Tryptone | 7g |
| Soya peptone | 2.3g |
| Sodium chloride | 2.3g |
| Calcium carbonate | 25g |
| Sodium thiosulphate ($Na_2S_2O_3 . 5H_2O$) | 40.7g |
| Ox bile | 4.75g |
| Distilled water | 1000ml |

Dissolve the ingredients and then add the calcium carbonate. Shake well and dispense in bottles. Autoclave at 115°C for 10 minutes.

Iodine solution:

| | |
|---|---|
| Iodine | 20g |
| Potassium iodide | 25g |
| Distilled water | 100ml |

Dissolve the potassium iodide in a little of the distilled water. Add the iodine and shake vigorously. Add the rest of the water, a little at a time.

Brilliant-green solution:

| | |
|---|---|
| Brilliant-green | 0.1g |
| Distilled water | 100ml |

Add the brilliant-green to the distilled water and shake to dissolve the dye. Heat the solution to 100°C for 30 minutes, and shake from time to time whilst cooling to ensure that the dye has dissolved completely. Store in a brown glass bottle in the dark.

Preparation of complete medium:

For use, add to each 100ml of broth base exactly 1.9ml of iodine solution and 0.95ml of brilliant-green solution. Mix and distribute in sterile containers as required.

## Xylose Lysine Deoxycholate (XLD) Agar (Taylor, 1965)

Basal medium:

| | |
|---|---|
| Lactose | 7.5g |
| Sucrose | 7.5g |
| Xylose | 3.75g |
| L(-)Lysine hydrochloride | 5g |
| Sodium chloride | 5g |
| Yeast extract | 3g |
| Phenol red (0.4 per cent w/v aqueous solution) | 20ml |
| Agar | 12g |
| Distilled water | 1000ml |

Steam to dissolve ingredients and distribute in screw-capped bottles. Autoclave at 115°C for 10 minutes.

Solution A

| | |
|---|---|
| Sodium thiosulphate ($Na_2S_2O_3 . 5H_2O$) | 34g |
| Ferric ammonium citrate | 4g |
| Distilled water | 100ml |

Heat gently to dissolve. Pasteurize at 60°C for 1 hour.

Solution B

| | |
|---|---|
| Sodium deoxycholate | 10g |
| Distilled water | 100ml |

Dissolve and pasteurize at 60°C for one hour.

Final Medium

For use, melt the basal medium, cool to approximately 50°C, and add aseptically 2.0ml of Solution A per 100ml of basal medium. Mix gently. With a separate pipette, add aseptically 2.5ml of Solution B per 100ml of basal medium. Mix, and pour into Petri dishes. The final pH should be 7.3.

79

### Lysine Iron Agar (Edwards and Fife, 1961)

| | |
|---|---|
| Peptone | 5g |
| Yeast extract | 3g |
| Glucose | 1g |
| L(-)Lysine | 10g |
| Ferric ammonium citrate | 0.5g |
| Sodium thiosulphate ($Na_2S_2O_3.5H_2O$) | 0.04g |
| Bromocresol purple | 0.02g |
| Agar | 14.5g |
| Distilled water | 1000ml |

Steam to dissolve ingredients and then dispense in 5ml volumes in small test tubes (150x12mm). Autoclave at 115°C for 10 minutes. Cool in a sloping position to give agar slopes with a deep butt. The final pH should be approximately 6.7. No adjustment is usually necessary.

### Triple Sugar Iron Agar (IAMS, 1958)

| | |
|---|---|
| Lab-Lemco | 3g |
| Yeast extract | 3g |
| Peptone | 20g |
| Sodium chloride | 5g |
| Lactose | 10g |
| Sucrose | 10g |
| Glucose | 1g |
| Ferric citrate | 0.3g |
| Sodium thiosulphate ($Na_2S_2O_3.5H_2O$) | 0.3g |
| Phenol red (0.4 per cent w/v aqueous solution) | 6ml |
| Agar | 15g |
| Distilled water to | 1000ml |

Steam to dissolve ingredients. Add the indicator and dispense in 5ml volumes into small test tubes (150x12mm) and autoclave at 115°C for 10 minutes. Cool in a sloping position to form a slope with a deep butt. The final pH should be approximately 7.4. No adjustment is usually necessary.

### Urea Broth

Broth base:

| | |
|---|---|
| Peptone | 1g |
| Glucose | 1g |
| Disodium hydrogen phosphate | 1g |
| Potassium dihydrogen phosphate | 0.8g |
| Sodium chloride | 5g |
| Phenol red (0.4 per cent w/v aqueous solution) | 1ml |
| Distilled water | 1000ml |

Dissolve the ingredients and check that the pH is approximately 6.8. Dispense in 95ml volumes in screw-capped bottles and autoclave at 115°C for 10 minutes.

For use, add aseptically 5ml of 40 per cent (w/v) solution of urea sterilized by filtration to 95ml Broth Base. Dispense aseptically in 2-3ml volumes in sterile bijou bottles.

# REAGENTS

## Kovacs' Reagent for Indole (Kovacs, 1928)

| | |
|---|---|
| Paradimethylaminobenzaldehyde | 5g |
| Amyl alcohol (AR and free from organic bases) | 75ml |
| Hydrochloric acid (concentrated) | 25ml |

Dissolve the aldehyde in the alcohol. Add the concentrated acid with care. Protect from light and store at 4°C.

NOTE: The reagent should be light yellow to light brown in colour; some samples of amyl alcohol are unsatisfactory, and give a dark colour with the aldehyde.

## Oxidase Reagent

| | |
|---|---|
| Tetramethyl-p-phenylenediamine hydrochloride | 0.1g |
| Distilled water | 10ml |

This reagent does not keep and it must therefore be freshly prepared for use in small amounts each time that it is needed.

## Ringer's Solution (Quarter-strength)

| | |
|---|---|
| Sodium chloride | 2.25g |
| Potassium chloride | 0.105g |
| Calcium chloride, anhydrous | 0.12g |
| Sodium bicarbonate | 0.05g |
| Distilled water | 1000ml |

Dissolve the ingredients and dispense in convenient volumes. Sterilize by autoclaving at 121°C for 15 minutes.

## Filter-Aid (Hammarström and Ljutov, 1954)

| | |
|---|---|
| Hyflo-supercel (BDH 33216) | approx 1g |
| Distilled water | 15ml |

Add the filter aid to the water in a screw-capped universal bottle and autoclave at 121°C for 15 minutes. Prepare several bottles at the same time and store until required.

# Appendix C

## Tables of Most Probable Numbers

These tables indicate, from the various combinations of positive and negative reactions for the different volumes of water examined, the estimated number of bacteria of the type sought in 100ml of the sample. It is important to realise that this, the most probable number (MPN), is only an estimate based on statistical probability and that the true number will usually lie within a calculated range of the MPN value. Table 4 and Table 5 give 95 per cent confidence limits for test series containing 50ml volumes when used for water samples. In Table 6, all the possible combinations of positive and negative reactions are listed and 95 per cent confidence limits are given where applicable. The combinations for which confidence limits are not shown are less likely and if these should occur in practice with a frequency greater than about 1 in 100 tests, it is an indication that the statistical assumptions underlying the MPN estimation are not being fulfilled (Swaroop, 1951; Woodward, 1957; de Man, 1975). For example, the organisms may not have been uniformly distributed throughout the sample or toxic substances may have been present. The 95 per cent confidence limits are calculated on the basis of statistical considerations alone. They do not take account of variability, due to non-random distribution of organisms in the water as sampled or during preparation of the sample for analysis.

## Calculation of MPN Values

Record the number of positive reactions for each set of tubes and, from the relevant MPN table, read the most probable number of organisms present in 100ml of the sample.

Where a series of dilutions of the sample are used, apply the following rules:

i. Use only three consecutive sets of dilutions for calculation of the MPN value.

ii. Where a series of dilutions has been used, select the smallest sample volume giving some positive reactions together with the two preceding sets of dilutions (See Examples a and b).

Multiply the value derived from the table by the dilution factor used to give the estimated number of organisms per 100 ml.

iii. Wherever possible, use sets of dilutions in which the results are neither all positive nor all negative. Where this is not possible, choose sets of dilutions containing positive rather than all negative reactions (See Example c).

iv.  If less than three sets of dilutions give positive results, start with the set containing the largest volume of the sample (see Example d).

v.  If only one set of tubes gives a positive reaction, use this dilution and the one higher and one lower (see Example e).

---

Examples of the derivation of Most Probable Numbers from the numbers of positive reactions in sets of five tubes.*

| Example in text | Volume of sample | | | | | MPN per 100ml |
|:---:|:---:|:---:|:---:|:---:|:---:|:---:|
| | 10ml | 1ml | 0.1ml | 0.01ml | 0.001ml | |
| a | **5** | **3** | **2** | 0 | | 140 |
| b | 5 | **5** | **3** | **2** | 0 | 1400 |
| c | **5** | **5** | **2** | 0 | 0 | 540 |
| d | **3** | **1** | **0** | 0 | | 11 |
| e | **0** | **1** | **0** | 0 | | 2 |

*Numbers in bold type indicate which results should be used in determining the MPN values.

83

Table 4. MPN values per 100ml of sample and 95 per cent confidence limits for a set of one 50ml and five 10ml volumes.

| Number of tubes giving a positive reaction | | MPN | 95 per cent Confidence Limits | |
|---|---|---|---|---|
| 1 x 50ml | 5 x 10ml | per 100ml | lower | upper |
| 0 | 0 | <1 | | |
| 0 | 1 | 1 | 0.5 — | 4 |
| 0 | 2 | 2 | 0.5 — | 6 |
| 0 | 3 | 4 | 0.5 — | 11 |
| 0 | 4 | 5 | 1 — | 13 |
| 0 | 5 | 7 | 2 — | 17 |
| 1 | 0 | 2 | 0.5 — | 6 |
| 1 | 1 | 3 | 0.5 — | 9 |
| 1 | 2 | 6 | 1 — | 15 |
| 1 | 3 | 9 | 2 — | 21 |
| 1 | 4 | 16 | 4 — | 40 |
| 1 | 5 | >18 | | |

Table 5.    MPN values per 100ml of sample and 95 per cent confidence limits for a set of one 50ml, five 10ml volumes and five 1ml volumes.

| Number of tubes giving a positive reaction | | | MPN | 95 per cent Confidence Limits | |
|---|---|---|---|---|---|
| 1 x 50ml | 5 x 10ml | 5 x 1ml | per 100ml | lower | upper |
| 0 | 0 | 0 | <1 | | |
| 0 | 0 | 1 | 1 | 0.5 — | 4 |
| 0 | 0 | 2 | 2 | 0.5 — | 6 |
| 0 | 1 | 0 | 1 | 0.5 — | 4 |
| 0 | 1 | 1 | 2 | 0.5 — | 6 |
| 0 | 1 | 2 | 3 | 0.5 — | 8 |
| 0 | 2 | 0 | 2 | 0.5 — | 6 |
| 0 | 2 | 1 | 3 | 0.5 — | 8 |
| 0 | 2 | 2 | 4 | 0.5 — | 11 |
| 0 | 3 | 0 | 3 | 0.5 — | 8 |
| 0 | 3 | 1 | 5 | 0.5 — | 13 |
| 0 | 4 | 0 | 5 | 0.5 — | 13 |
| 1 | 0 | 0 | 1 | 0.5 — | 4 |
| 1 | 0 | 1 | 3 | 0.5 — | 8 |
| 1 | 0 | 2 | 4 | 0.5 — | 11 |
| 1 | 0 | 3 | 6 | 0.5 — | 15 |
| 1 | 1 | 0 | 3 | 0.5 — | 8 |
| 1 | 1 | 1 | 5 | 0.5 — | 13 |
| 1 | 1 | 2 | 7 | 1 — | 17 |
| 1 | 1 | 3 | 9 | 2 — | 21 |
| 1 | 2 | 0 | 5 | 0.5 — | 13 |
| 1 | 2 | 1 | 7 | 1 — | 17 |
| 1 | 2 | 2 | 10 | 3 — | 23 |
| 1 | 2 | 3 | 12 | 3 — | 28 |
| 1 | 3 | 0 | 8 | 2 — | 19 |
| 1 | 3 | 1 | 11 | 3 — | 26 |
| 1 | 3 | 2 | 14 | 4 — | 34 |
| 1 | 3 | 3 | 18 | 5 — | 53 |
| 1 | 3 | 4 | 21 | 6 — | 66 |
| 1 | 4 | 0 | 13 | 4 — | 31 |
| 1 | 4 | 1 | 17 | 5 — | 47 |
| 1 | 4 | 2 | 22 | 7 — | 69 |
| 1 | 4 | 3 | 28 | 9 — | 85 |
| 1 | 4 | 4 | 35 | 12 — | 101 |
| 1 | 4 | 5 | 43 | 15 — | 117 |
| 1 | 5 | 0 | 24 | 8 — | 75 |
| 1 | 5 | 1 | 35 | 12 — | 101 |
| 1 | 5 | 2 | 54 | 18 — | 138 |
| 1 | 5 | 3 | 92 | 27 — | 217 |
| 1 | 5 | 4 | 161 | 3 — | 450 |
| 1 | 5 | 5 | >180 | | |

Table 6.  MPN values per 100ml of sample and 95 per cent confidence limits where appropriate for three sets of five tubes containing 10ml, 1ml and 0.1ml test volumes respectively.

| Number of tubes giving a positive reaction | | | MPN per 100ml | 95 per cent Confidence Limits | |
|---|---|---|---|---|---|
| 10 ml | 1 ml | 0.1 ml | | lower | upper |
| 0 | 0 | 0 | <2 | 0.5 | 7 |
|   |   | 1 | 2 |   |   |
|   |   | 2 | 4 |   |   |
|   |   | 3 | 5 |   |   |
|   |   | 4 | 7 |   |   |
|   |   | 5 | 9 |   |   |
| 0 | 1 | 0 | 2 | 0.5 | 7 |
|   |   | 1 | 4 |   |   |
|   |   | 2 | 6 |   |   |
|   |   | 3 | 7 |   |   |
|   |   | 4 | 9 |   |   |
|   |   | 5 | 11 |   |   |
| 0 | 2 | 0 | 4 | 0.5 | 11 |
|   |   | 1 | 6 |   |   |
|   |   | 2 | 7 |   |   |
|   |   | 3 | 9 |   |   |
|   |   | 4 | 11 |   |   |
|   |   | 5 | 13 |   |   |
| 0 | 3 | 0 | 6 |   |   |
|   |   | 1 | 7 |   |   |
|   |   | 2 | 9 |   |   |
|   |   | 3 | 11 |   |   |
|   |   | 4 | 13 |   |   |
|   |   | 5 | 15 |   |   |
| 0 | 4 | 0 | 8 |   |   |
|   |   | 1 | 9 |   |   |
|   |   | 2 | 11 |   |   |
|   |   | 3 | 13 |   |   |
|   |   | 4 | 15 |   |   |
|   |   | 5 | 17 |   |   |
| 0 | 5 | 0 | 9 |   |   |
|   |   | 1 | 11 |   |   |
|   |   | 2 | 13 |   |   |
|   |   | 3 | 15 |   |   |
|   |   | 4 | 17 |   |   |
|   |   | 5 | 19 |   |   |

Table 6 continued

| Number of tubes giving a positive reaction | | | MPN per 100ml | 95 per cent Confidence Limits | |
|---|---|---|---|---|---|
| 10 ml | 1 ml | 0.1 ml | | lower | upper |
| 1 | 0 | 0 | 2 | 0.5 — | 7 |
| | | 1 | 4 | 0.5 — | 11 |
| | | 2 | 6 | | |
| | | 3 | 8 | | |
| | | 4 | 10 | | |
| | | 5 | 12 | | |
| 1 | 1 | 0 | 4 | 0.5 — | 11 |
| | | 1 | 6 | 0.5 — | 15 |
| | | 2 | 8 | | |
| | | 3 | 10 | | |
| | | 4 | 12 | | |
| | | 5 | 14 | | |
| 1 | 2 | 0 | 6 | 0.5 — | 15 |
| | | 1 | 8 | | |
| | | 2 | 10 | | |
| | | 3 | 12 | | |
| | | 4 | 15 | | |
| | | 5 | 17 | | |
| 1 | 3 | 0 | 8 | | |
| | | 1 | 10 | | |
| | | 2 | 13 | | |
| | | 3 | 15 | | |
| | | 4 | 17 | | |
| | | 5 | 19 | | |
| 1 | 4 | 0 | 11 | | |
| | | 1 | 13 | | |
| | | 2 | 15 | | |
| | | 3 | 17 | | |
| | | 4 | 19 | | |
| | | 5 | 22 | | |
| 1 | 5 | 0 | 13 | | |
| | | 1 | 15 | | |
| | | 2 | 17 | | |
| | | 3 | 19 | | |
| | | 4 | 22 | | |
| | | 5 | 24 | | |

# Table 6 continued

| Number of tubes giving a positive reaction | | | MPN per 100 ml | 95 per cent Confidence Limits | |
|---|---|---|---|---|---|
| 10 ml | 1 ml | 0.1 ml | | lower | upper |
| 2 | 0 | 0 | 5 | 0.5 — | 13 |
|   |   | 1 | 7 | 1 — | 17 |
|   |   | 2 | 9 | | |
|   |   | 3 | 12 | | |
|   |   | 4 | 14 | | |
|   |   | 5 | 16 | | |
| 2 | 1 | 0 | 7 | 1 — | 17 |
|   |   | 1 | 9 | 2 — | 21 |
|   |   | 2 | 12 | | |
|   |   | 3 | 14 | | |
|   |   | 4 | 17 | | |
|   |   | 5 | 19 | | |
| 2 | 2 | 0 | 9 | 2 — | 21 |
|   |   | 1 | 12 | | |
|   |   | 2 | 14 | | |
|   |   | 3 | 17 | | |
|   |   | 4 | 19 | | |
|   |   | 5 | 22 | | |
| 2 | 3 | 0 | 12 | 3 — | 28 |
|   |   | 1 | 14 | | |
|   |   | 2 | 17 | | |
|   |   | 3 | 20 | | |
|   |   | 4 | 22 | | |
|   |   | 5 | 25 | | |
| 2 | 4 | 0 | 15 | | |
|   |   | 1 | 17 | | |
|   |   | 2 | 20 | | |
|   |   | 3 | 23 | | |
|   |   | 4 | 25 | | |
|   |   | 5 | 28 | | |
| 2 | 5 | 0 | 17 | | |
|   |   | 1 | 20 | | |
|   |   | 2 | 23 | | |
|   |   | 3 | 26 | | |
|   |   | 4 | 29 | | |
|   |   | 5 | 32 | | |

Table 6 continued

| Number of tubes giving a positive reaction | | | MPN per 100 ml | 95 per cent Confidence Limits | |
|---|---|---|---|---|---|
| 10 ml | 1 ml | 0.1 ml | | lower | upper |
| 3 | 0 | 0 | 8 | 1 — 19 | |
|   |   | 1 | 11 | 2 — 25 | |
|   |   | 2 | 13 |   |   |
|   |   | 3 | 16 |   |   |
|   |   | 4 | 20 |   |   |
|   |   | 5 | 23 |   |   |
| 3 | 1 | 0 | 11 | 2 — 25 | |
|   |   | 1 | 14 | 4 — 34 | |
|   |   | 2 | 17 |   |   |
|   |   | 3 | 20 |   |   |
|   |   | 4 | 23 |   |   |
|   |   | 5 | 27 |   |   |
| 3 | 2 | 0 | 14 | 4 — 34 | |
|   |   | 1 | 17 | 5 — 46 | |
|   |   | 2 | 20 |   |   |
|   |   | 3 | 24 |   |   |
|   |   | 4 | 27 |   |   |
|   |   | 5 | 31 |   |   |
| 3 | 3 | 0 | 17 | 5 — 46 | |
|   |   | 1 | 21 |   |   |
|   |   | 2 | 24 |   |   |
|   |   | 3 | 28 |   |   |
|   |   | 4 | 31 |   |   |
|   |   | 5 | 35 |   |   |
| 3 | 4 | 0 | 21 |   |   |
|   |   | 1 | 24 |   |   |
|   |   | 2 | 28 |   |   |
|   |   | 3 | 32 |   |   |
|   |   | 4 | 36 |   |   |
|   |   | 5 | 40 |   |   |
| 3 | 5 | 0 | 25 |   |   |
|   |   | 1 | 29 |   |   |
|   |   | 2 | 32 |   |   |
|   |   | 3 | 37 |   |   |
|   |   | 4 | 41 |   |   |
|   |   | 5 | 45 |   |   |

Table 6 continued

| Number of tubes giving a positive reaction | | | MPN per 100ml | 95 per cent Confidence Limits | | |
|---|---|---|---|---|---|---|
| 10 ml | 1 ml | 0.1 ml | | lower | | upper |
| 4 | 0 | 0 | 13 | 3 | — | 31 |
|   |   | 1 | 17 | 5 | — | 46 |
|   |   | 2 | 21 |   |   |   |
|   |   | 3 | 25 |   |   |   |
|   |   | 4 | 30 |   |   |   |
|   |   | 5 | 36 |   |   |   |
| 4 | 1 | 0 | 17 | 5 | — | 46 |
|   |   | 1 | 21 | 7 | — | 63 |
|   |   | 2 | 26 | 9 | — | 78 |
|   |   | 3 | 31 |   |   |   |
|   |   | 4 | 36 |   |   |   |
|   |   | 5 | 42 |   |   |   |
| 4 | 2 | 0 | 22 | 7 | — | 67 |
|   |   | 1 | 26 | 9 | — | 78 |
|   |   | 2 | 32 |   |   |   |
|   |   | 3 | 38 |   |   |   |
|   |   | 4 | 44 |   |   |   |
|   |   | 5 | 50 |   |   |   |
| 4 | 3 | 0 | 27 | 9 | — | 80 |
|   |   | 1 | 33 | 11 | — | 93 |
|   |   | 2 | 39 |   |   |   |
|   |   | 3 | 45 |   |   |   |
|   |   | 4 | 52 |   |   |   |
|   |   | 5 | 59 |   |   |   |
| 4 | 4 | 0 | 34 | 12 | — | 93 |
|   |   | 1 | 40 |   |   |   |
|   |   | 2 | 47 |   |   |   |
|   |   | 3 | 54 |   |   |   |
|   |   | 4 | 62 |   |   |   |
|   |   | 5 | 69 |   |   |   |
| 4 | 5 | 0 | 41 |   |   |   |
|   |   | 1 | 48 |   |   |   |
|   |   | 2 | 56 |   |   |   |
|   |   | 3 | 64 |   |   |   |
|   |   | 4 | 72 |   |   |   |
|   |   | 5 | 81 |   |   |   |

# Table 6 continued

| Number of tubes giving a positive reaction | | | MPN per 100ml | 95 per cent Confidence Limits | |
|---|---|---|---|---|---|
| 10 ml | 1 ml | 0.1 ml | | lower | upper |
| 5 | 0 | 0 | 23 | 7 — | 70 |
| | | 1 | 31 | 11 — | 89 |
| | | 2 | 43 | 15 — | 110 |
| | | 3 | 58 | | |
| | | 4 | 76 | | |
| | | 5 | 95 | | |
| 5 | 1 | 0 | 33 | 11 — | 93 |
| | | 1 | 46 | 16 — | 120 |
| | | 2 | 63 | 21 — | 150 |
| | | 3 | 84 | | |
| | | 4 | 110 | | |
| | | 5 | 130 | | |
| 5 | 2 | 0 | 49 | 17 — | 130 |
| | | 1 | 70 | 23 — | 170 |
| | | 2 | 94 | 28 — | 220 |
| | | 3 | 120 | | |
| | | 4 | 150 | | |
| | | 5 | 180 | | |
| 5 | 3 | 0 | 79 | 25 — | 190 |
| | | 1 | 110 | 31 — | 250 |
| | | 2 | 140 | 37 — | 340 |
| | | 3 | 180 | 44 — | 500 |
| | | 4 | 210 | | |
| | | 5 | 250 | | |
| 5 | 4 | 0 | 130 | 35 — | 300 |
| | | 1 | 170 | 43 — | 490 |
| | | 2 | 220 | 57 — | 700 |
| | | 3 | 280 | 90 — | 850 |
| | | 4 | 350 | 120 — | 1000 |
| | | 5 | 430 | | |
| 5 | 5 | 0 | 240 | 68 — | 750 |
| | | 1 | 350 | 120 — | 1000 |
| | | 2 | 540 | 180 — | 1400 |
| | | 3 | 920 | 300 — | 3200 |
| | | 4 | 1600 | 640 — | 5800 |
| | | 5 | >1800 | — | |

# References

List of Abbreviations used:

APHA    American Public Health Association
BSI    British Standards Institution
CDSC    PHLS Communicable Disease Surveillance Centre
DHSS    Department of Health and Social Security
EEC    European Economic Community
IAMS    International Association of Microbiological Societies
NWC    National Water Council
PHLS    Public Health Laboratory Service
SCA    Standing Committee of Analysts
WHO    World Health Organization

ALLEN, L.A., PIERCE, M.A.F. & SMITH, H.M. (1953) Enumeration of *Streptococcus faecalis*, with particular reference to polluted waters. *Journal of Hygiene*, **51**, 458.
APHA (1976) *Standard methods for the examination of water and waste water*, 14th edn, p. 893. Washington D.C., American Public Health Association.

BARROW, G.I., MILLER, D.C., GRAY, R.D. & LOWE, G.H. (1978) *Report of a feasibility study on the distribution and use of simulated water samples for comparative bacteriological analysis.* Luxembourg, Office for Official Publications of the European Communities, 1978. (EUR 6037).
BROWN, M.W.R. & FOSTER, J.H.S. (1970) A simple diagnostic milk medium for *Pseudomonas aeruginosa. Journal of Clinical Pathology*, **23**, 172.
BSI (1982) *Specification of requirements for suitability of materials for use in contact with water for human consumption with regard to their effect on the quality of the water.* Draft for Development DD82. British Standards Institution, London.
BURMAN, N.P. (1955) The standardization and selection of bile salt and peptone for culture media used in the bacteriological examination of water. *Proceedings of the Society for Water Treatment and Examination*, **4**, 10.
BURMAN, N.P., OLIVER, C.W. & STEVENS, J.K. (1969) Membrane filtration techniques for the isolation from water of coli-aerogenes, *Escherichia coli*, faecal streptococci, *Clostridium perfringens*, actinomycetes and microfungi. In: *Isolation methods for microbiologists*, edited by D.A. Shapton & G.W. Gould. p. 127. London. Academic Press. (Society for Applied Bacteriology Technical Series No.3).

CLARKE, P.H. (1953) Growth of streptococci in a glucose phenolphthalein broth. *Journal of General Microbiology*, **9**, 350.

COCHRAN, W.G. (1950) Estimation of bacterial densities by means of "the most probable number". *Biometrics,* **6,** 105.

COLLINS, C.H., HARTLEY, E.G. & PILSWORTH, R. (1974) *The prevention of laboratory acquired infection.* London, HMSO (PHLS Monograph Series No. 6).

COOK, G. T. (1952) Comparison of two modifications of bismuth-sulphite agar for the isolation and growth of *Salmonella typhi* and *Salm. typhi-murium. Journal of Pathology and Bacteriology,* **64,** 559.

COWAN, S.T. (1974) *Cowan and Steel's Manual for the Identification of Medical Bacteria.* 2nd Edn. London, Cambridge University Press.

COX, C.R. (1964) *Operation and control of water treatment processes.* Geneva, World Health Organization. (WHO Monograph Series No. 49).

DHSS *et al.* (1969) *The bacteriological examination of water supplies,* 4th Edn. (Department of Health and Social Security, Department of the Environment and the Welsh Office : Reports on public health and medical subjects No. 71). London, HMSO.

DHSS *et al.* (1978) *Code of practice for the prevention of infection in clinical laboratories and post mortem rooms* (Chairman of working party : Sir James Howie). Department of Health and Social Security, Scottish Home and Health Department, Department of Health and Social Services Northern Ireland and Welsh Office. London, HMSO.

DRAKE, C.H. (1966) Evaluation of culture media for the isolation and enumeration of *Pseudomonas aeruginosa. Health Laboratory Science,* **3,** 10.

EDEL, W. & KAMPELMACHER, E.H. (1969) Salmonella isolation in nine European laboratories using a standardized technique. *Bulletin of the World Health Organization,* **41,** 297.

EDEL, W. & KAMPELMACHER, E.H. (1973) Comparative studies on the isolation of 'sublethally injured' salmonellae in nine European laboratories. *Bulletin of the World Health Organization,* **48,** 167.

EDWARDS, P.R. & EWING, W.H. (1972) *Identification of Enterobacteriaceae* 3rd edn. Minneapolis, Burgess.

EDWARDS, P.R. & FIFE, M.A. (1961) Lysine-iron agar in the detection of Arizona cultures. *Applied Microbiology,* **9,** 478.

EISENHART, C. & WILSON, P.W. (1943) Statistical methods and control in bacteriology. *Bacteriological Reviews,* **7,** 57.

EUROPEAN COMMUNITY (1975) Council Directive No. 75/440/EEC of 25 July 1975 concerning the quality required of surface water intended for abstraction of drinking water in member states. *Official Journal of the European Communities,* **No. L194,** 26.

EUROPEAN COMMUNITY (1979) Council Directive No. 79/869/EEC of 9 October 1979 on the quality of water for abstraction. *Official Journal of the European Communities,* **No. L271,** 44.

EUROPEAN COMMUNITY (1980a) Council Directive No. 80/777/EEC of 15 July 1980 on the approximation of the laws of the member states relating to the exploitation and marketing of natural mineral waters. *Official Journal of the European Communities,* **No. L229,** 1.

EUROPEAN COMMUNITY (1980b) Council Directive No. 80/778/EEC of 15 July 1980 relating to the quality of water intended for human consumption. *Official Journal of the European Communities,* **No. L229,** 11.

FENNELL, H. (1972) A single tube confirmatory test for *E. coli* at 44°C. *Water Treatment and Examination,* **21,** 13.

FOLPMERS, T. (1948) Is it justified to use lactose broth for the detection of *E. coli* in the presumptive test of routine water analysis? *Antonie van Leeuwenhoek,* **14,** 58.

GEIGY (1970) *Documenta Scientifica,* edited by K. Diem & C. Lentner, p.128, Macclesfield, Geigy Pharmaceuticals.

GIBBS, B.M. & FREAME, B. (1965) Methods for the recovery of clostridia from foods. *Journal of Applied Bacteriology,* **28,** 95.

GRAY, R.D. (1964) An improved formate lactose glutamate medium for the detection of *Escherichia coli* and other coliform organisms in water. *Journal of Hygiene,* **62,** 495.

HAIGHT, F.A. (1967) *Handbook of the Poisson Distribution,* London, John Wiley. (Publications in Operations Research No.11).

HAMMARSTRÖM, E. & LJUTOV, V. (1954) Concentration technique for demonstrating small amounts of bacteria in tap-water. *Acta Pathologica et Microbiologica Scandinavica,* **35,** 365.

HANNAY, C.L. & NORTON, I.L. (1947) Enumeration, isolation and study of faecal streptococci from river water. *Proceedings of the Society for Applied Bacteriology,* **No. 1,** 39.

HARVEY, R.W.S. (1956) Choice of a selective medium for the routine isolation of members of the Salmonella group. *Monthly Bulletin of the Ministry of Health and the Public Health Laboratory Service,* **15,** 118.

HARVEY, R.W.S. & PRICE, T.H. (1974) *Isolation of Salmonellas,* London, HMSO, (PHLS Monograph Series No. 8).

HARVEY, R.W.S. & PRICE, T.H. (1977) Observations on pre-enrichment for isolating salmonellas from sewage polluted natural water using Muller-Kauffmann tetrathionate broth prepared with fresh and desiccated ox bile. *Journal of Applied Bacteriology,* **43,** 145.

HARVEY, R.W.S. & PRICE, T.H. (1979) A review : principles of Salmonella isolation. *Journal of Applied Bacteriology,* **46,** 27.

HARVEY, R.W.S. & PRICE, T.H. (1980) Salmonella isolation with Rappaport's medium after pre-enrichment in buffered peptone water using a series of inoculum ratios. *Journal of Hygiene,* **85,** 125.

HARVEY, R.W.S. & PRICE, T.H. (1981) Comparison of selenite F, Muller-Kauffmann tetrathionate and Rappaport's medium for Salmonella isolation from chicken giblets after pre-enrichment in buffered peptone water. *Journal of Hygiene,* **87,** 219.

HARVEY, R.W.S., PRICE, T.H. & HALL, M.L.M. (1973) Isolations of subgenus III salmonellas (arizonas) in Cardiff, 1959 — 1971. *Journal of Hygiene,* **71,** 481.

HARVEY, R.W.S., PRICE, T.H. & XIROUCHAKI, E. (1979) Comparison of selenite F, Muller-Kauffmann tetrathionate and Rappaport's medium for the isolation of salmonellas from sewage-polluted natural water using a pre-enrichment technique. *Journal of Hygiene*, **83**, 451.

HOBBS, B.C. & ALLISON, V.D. (1945a) Studies on the isolation of *Bact. typhosum* and *Bact. paratyphosum B*. Part I. *Monthly Bulletin of the Ministry of Health and the Public Health Laboratory Service*, **4**, 12.

HOBBS, B.C. & ALLISON, V.D. (1945b) Studies on the isolation of *Bact. typhosum* and *Bact. paratyphosum B*. Part III. *Monthly Bulletin of the Ministry of Health and the Public Health Laboratory Service*, **4**, 63.

HOLDEN, W.S. ed (1970) *Water treatment and examination*, p. 362. London, Churchill.

HOSKINS, J.K. (1934) Most probable numbers for evaluation of coli-aerogenes tests by fermentation tube method. *Public Health Reports, Washington*, **49**, 393.

HUGH, R. & LEIFSON, E. (1953) The taxonomic significance of fermentative versus oxidative metabolism of carbohydrates by various Gram negative bacteria. *Journal of Bacteriology*, **66**, 24.

HUTCHINSON, M. & RIDGWAY, J.W. (1977) Microbiological Aspects of Drinking Water Supplies. In : *Aquatic Microbiology*, edited by F.A. Skinner & J.M. Shewan, p. 179. London, Academic Press. (Society for Applied Bacteriology Symposium Series No. 6).

HYNES, M. (1942) The isolation of intestinal pathogens by selective media. *Journal of Pathology and Bacteriology*, **54**, 193.

IAMS (1958) Report of the Enterobacteriaeceae Subcommittee of the Nomenclature Committee of the International Association of Microbiological Societies. *International Bulletin of Bacterial Nomenclature and Taxonomy*, **8**, 25.

IVESON, J.B., KOVACS, N. & LAURIE, W. (1964) An improved method of isolating salmonellae from contaminated desiccated coconut. *Journal of Clinical Pathology*, **17**, 75.

JAMESON, J.E. (1963) A note on the isolation of salmonellae. *Journal of Applied Bacteriology*, **26**, 112.

JAMESON, J.E. & EMBERLEY, N.W. (1956) A substitute for bile salts in culture media. *Journal of general Microbiology*, **15**, 198.

KOSER, S.A. (1923) Utilization of the salts of organic acids by the colon-aerogenes group. *Journal of Bacteriology*, **8**, 493.

KOVÁCS, N. (1928) Eine vereinfachte Methode zum Nachweis der Indolbildung durch Bakterien. *Zeitschrift für Immunitätsforschung und experimentelle Therapie*, **55**, 311.

KOVÁCS, N. (1956) Identification of *Pseudomonas pyocyanea* by the oxidase reaction. *Nature, London*, **178**, 703.

LEIFSON, E. (1935) New culture media based on sodium deoxycholate for isolation of intestinal pathogens and for enumeration of colon bacilli in milk and water. *Journal of Pathology and Bacteriology*, **40**, 581.

LEIFSON, E. (1936) New selenite enrichment media for the isolation of typhoid and paratyphoid (Salmonella) bacilli. *American Journal of Hygiene*, **24**, 423.

LOUREIRO, J.A. de (1942) A modification of Wilson and Blair's bismuth sulphite agar (stabilized stock solutions). *Journal of Hygiene,* **42,** 224.

McCoy, J.H. (1962) The isolation of Salmonellae. *Journal of Applied Bacteriology,* **25,** 213.

McCRADY, M.H. (1915) The numerical interpretation of fermentation-tube results. *Journal of Infectious Diseases,* **17,** 183.

McCRADY, M.H. (1918) Tables for rapid interpretation of fermentation-tube results. *Public Health Journal, Toronto,* **9,** 201.

MAN, J.C. de (1975) The probability of most probable numbers. *European Journal of applied Microbiology,* **1,** 67.

MEAD, G.C. (1963) A medium for the isolation of *Streptococcus faecalis, sensu strictu. Nature, London,* **197,** 1323.

MEAD, G.C. (1964) Isolation and significance of *Streptococcus faecalis, sensu strictu. Nature, London,* **204,** 1224.

MEAD, G.C. (1966) Faecal streptococci in water supplies and the problem of selective isolation. *Proceedings of the Society for Water Treatment and Examination,* **15,** 207.

MOORE, B. (1948) The detection of paratyphoid carriers in towns by means of sewage examination. *Monthly Bulletin of the Ministry of Health and the Public Health Laboratory Service,* **7,** 241.

MOORE, B. (1950) The detection of typhoid carriers in towns by means of sewage examination. *Monthly Bulletin of the Ministry of Health and the Public Health Laboratory Service,* **9,** 72.

MOORE, B., PERRY, E.L. & CHARD, S.T. (1952) A survey by the sewage swab method of latent enteric infection in an urban area. *Journal of Hygiene,* **50,** 137.

NWC (1979) *Water supply hygiene : safeguards in the operation and management of public waterworks in England and Wales.* National Water Council. London, (NWC Occasional Technical Paper No. 2).
This Technical paper is also issued as SDD Memorandum 13/1979 by the Scottish Development Department, 47 Robb's Loan, Edinburgh, EH14 1TY.

NWC (1981a) Requirements for the testing of non-metallic materials for use in contact with potable water by the Fittings Scheme Technical Committee, *National Water Council, Bulletin 8,* Supplement 108D01. National Water Council, London.

NWC (1981b) *Guide to the microbiological implications of emergencies in the water service,* by the Microbiological Working Group, National Water Council, London.

NWC (1983) *Safety in microbiology laboratories in the water industry,* by the NWC Microbiological Working Group, National Water Council, London.

PANEZAI, A.K., MACKLIN, T.J. & COLES, H.G. (1965) Coli-aerogenes and *Escherichia coli* counts on water samples by means of transported membranes. *Proceedings of the Society for Water Treatment and Examination,* **14,** 179.

PHLS (1952) The effect of storage on the coliform and *Bacterium coli* counts of water samples : overnight storage at room and refrigerator temperature, by the Public Health Laboratory Service Water Sub-Committee *Journal of Hygiene,* **50,** 107.

PHLS (1953a) The effect of anaerobic spore-bearing organisms on the validity of the presumptive coliform test as used in the bacteriological examination of water, by the Public Health Laboratory Service Water Sub-committee. *Journal of Hygiene,* **51,** 268.

PHLS (1953b) The effect of sodium thiosulphate on the coliform and *Bacterium coli* counts of non-chlorinated water samples, by the Public Health Laboratory Service Water Sub-committee. *Journal of Hygiene,* **51,** 572.

PHLS (1953c) The effect of storage on the coliform and *Bacterium coli* counts of water samples : storage for six hours at room and refrigerator temperatures, by the Public Health Laboratory Service Water Sub-committee. *Journal of Hygiene,* **51,** 559.

PHLS (1968a) Comparison of MacConkey broth, Teepol broth and glutamic acid media for the enumeration of coliform organisms in water, by the Public Health Laboratory Service Standing Committee on the Bacteriological Examination of Water Supplies. *Journal of Hygiene,* **66,** 67.

PHLS (1968b) Confirmatory tests for coliform organisms, by the Public Health Laboratory Service Committee on the Bacteriological Examination of Water Supplies. *Journal of Hygiene,* **66,** 641.

PHLS (1969) A minerals-modified glutamate medium for the enumeration of coliform organisms in water, by the Public Health Laboratory Service Standing Committee on the Bacteriological Examination of Water Supplies. *Journal of Hygiene,* **67,** 367.

PHLS (1978) Waterborne infectious disease in Britain, by the Public Health Laboratory Service Standing Sub-committee on the Bacteriological Examination of Water Supplies. *Journal of Hygiene,* **81,** 139.

PHLS & SCA (1980a) A comparison between minerals-modified glutamate medium and lauryl tryptose lactose broth for the enumeration of *Escherichia coli* and coliform organisms in water by the multiple tube method, by a Joint Committee of the Public Health Laboratory Service and the Standing Committee of Analysts. *Journal of Hygiene,* **85,** 35.

PHLS & SCA (1980b) Membrane filtration media for the enumeration of coliform organisms and *Escherichia coli* in water : comparison of Tergitol 7 and lauryl sulphate with Teepol 610, by a Joint Committee of the Public Health Laboratory Service and the Standing Committee of Analysts. *Journal of Hygiene,* **85,** 181.

PHLS & SCA (1980c) Single tube confirmatory tests for *Escherichia coli,* by a Joint Committee of the Public Health Laboratory Service and the Standing Committee of Analysts, *Journal of Hygiene,* **85,** 51.

PHLS & SCA (1981) A comparison of confirmatory media for coliform organisms and *Escherichia coli* in water, by a Joint Committee of the Public Health Laboratory Service and the Standing Committee of Analysts. *Journal of Hygiene,* **87,** 369.

PUGSLEY, A.P., EVISON, L.M. & JAMES, A. (1973). A simple technique for the differentiation of *Escherichia coli* in water examination. *Water Research,* **7,** 1431.

RAPPAPORT, F., KONFORTI, N. & NAVON, B. (1956) A new enrichment medium for certain salmonellae. *Journal of Clinical Pathology*, 9, 261.

SCA (1980) *Chemical disinfecting agents in water and effluents, and chlorine demand 1980*, by the Standing Committee of Analysts of the Department of the Environment and the National Water Council, London, HMSO. (Methods for the Examination of Water and Associated Materials).

SCA (1983) *Methods for the isolation and identification of Salmonellae (other than Salmonella typhi) from water and associated materials 1982*, by the Standing Committee of Analysts of the Department of the Environment and the National Water Council. London, HMSO. (Methods for the Examination of Water and Associated Materials).

SCHUBERT, R. (1956) Die coliformer Bakterien in der Wasserdiagnostik und ihre Differenzierungen. *Zeitschrift für Hygiene und Infektionskrankheiten*, 142, 476.

SCHUBERT, R. (1958) Studien zur Differenzierung coliformer Bakterien in der Wasserdiagnostik. *Zeitschrift für Hygiene und Infektionskrankheiten*, 144, 485.

SIMMONS, J.S. (1926) A culture medium for differentiating organisms of typhoid-colon aerogenes groups and for isolation of certain fungi. *Journal of Infectious Diseases*, 39, 209.

SKEAT, W.O. ed. (1969) *Manual of British water engineering practice*, 4th edn. Vol. III p. 180. London, Heffer.

SLANETZ, L.W. & BARTLEY, C.H. (1957). Numbers of enterococci in water, sewage and faeces determined by the membrane filter technique with an improved medium. *Journal of Bacteriology*, 74, 591.

SWAROOP, S. (1938). Numerical estimation of *B. coli* by dilution method. *Indian Journal of Medical Research*, 26, 353.

SWAROOP, S. (1951). The range of variation of the most probable number of organisms estimated by the dilution method. *Indian Journal of Medical Research*, 39, 107.

TAYLOR, E.W. (1955) Comparison of 6-hour and 24-hour incubation periods at 44°C as a confirmatory test for *Bacterium coli* Type 1. *Journal of Hygiene*, 53, 50.

TAYLOR, E.W. & WHISKIN, L.C. (1951) The disinfection of water mains after laying and carrying out repairs. *Journal of the Institution of Water Engineers*, 5, 219.

TAYLOR, W.I. & HARRIS, B. (1965) Isolation of Shigellae 1. Xylose lysine agars : new media for isolation of enteric pathogens. *American Journal of Clinical Pathology*, 44, 471.

VASSILIADIS, P., TRICHOPOULOS, D., PAPADAKIS, J. & POLITI, G. (1970) Salmonella isolations in abattoirs in Greece. *Journal of Hygiene*, 69, 601.

WHO (1971) *International standards for drinking water,* 3rd Edn. Geneva, World Health Organization.

WILSON, G.S., TWIGG, R.S., WRIGHT, R.C., HENDRY, C.B., COWELL, M.P. & MAIER, I. (1935). *The bacteriological grading of milk,* p.155. London, HMSO (Special Report Series of the Medical Research Council No. 206).

WILSON, W.J. & BLAIR, E.M.Mc.V. (1927). Use of glucose bismuth sulphite iron medium for the isolation of *B. typhosus* and *B. proteus. Journal of Hygiene,* **26,** 374.

WOODWARD, R.L. (1957). How probable is the most probable number? *Journal – American Water Works Association,* **49,** 1060.

# Index

   105

106

Printed in the UK for HMSO. Dd 737634   C15   8/84

**Public Health Laboratory Service and the Standing Committee of Analysts**

Members of the joint Panel associated with this Report

Dr. G.I. Barrow, PHLS, *(Chairman)*
Mr. A.W.J. Bufton, DOE
Dr. R.H.G. Charles, DHSS
Dr. J. Dadswell, PHLS
Mr. H. Fennell, Yorkshire Water
Dr. R.D. Gray, PHLS *(Deceased)*
Dr. M. Hutchinson, South West Water
Dr. F.B. Jackson, PHLS
Mr. F. Jones, North West Water
Dr. M.J. Lewis, PHLS
Mr. G.H. Lowe, PHLS
Dr. J.W. Ridgway, Water Research Centre
Dr. J.A. Rycroft, PHLS
Miss J.K. Stevens, Thames Water
Dr. H.E. Tillett, PHLS *(Statistician)*
Dr. J.G. Wallace, PHLS
Miss J. M. Watkinson, PHLS
Dr. A. E. Wright, PHLS

Chairman SCA Main Committee
Mr. T.A. Dick, DOE
Secretary SCA Main Committee
Mr. L.R. Pittwell, DOE

**Addresses for Correspondence**

Corrections, comments and other correspondence should be addressed to:

The Secretary,
Water Committee,
Public Health Laboratory Service,
61 Colindale Avenue,
LONDON NW9 5EQ.
England

The Secretary,
Standing Committee of Analysts,
Department of the Environment,
Romney House,
43 Marsham Street,
LONDON SW1P 3PY.
England